ELISSA TABAK-LOMBARDO

THE
Caring Parent's
Guide to Child Care

Everything You Need to Know
About Making Child Care Centers
Work for You and Your Child

PRIMA PUBLISHING

PRIMA PUBLISHING and colophon are registered trademarks of Prima Communications, Inc.

Illustrations by Rachel Anchors. Illustrations © 1999 Prima Publishing. All rights reserved.

To contact Elissa Tabak-Lombardo, visit her Web site at www.caringparent.com.

All products mentioned in this book are trademarks of their respective companies.

Library of Congress Cataloging-in-Publication Data on File

ISBN 0-7615-1710-3

99 00 01 02 03 BB 10 9 8 7 6 5 4 3 2 1
Printed in the United States of America

How to Order
Single copies may be ordered from Prima Publishing, P.O. Box 1260BK, Rocklin, CA 95677; telephone (916) 632-4400. Quantity discounts are also available. On your letterhead, include information concerning the intended use of the books and the number of books you wish to purchase.

Visit us online at www.primalife.com

CONTENTS

*This book is dedicated with love
to my grandmother,
and the memory of my grandfather.*

Rose and Sam Hodes

ACKNOWLEDGEMENTS

Over the years—long before I ever could have dreamed a book would be the evolution—parents, teachers, and caregivers generously shared their experiences with me. I have learned so much from each of these people, and I am grateful for the candor in which these anecdotes made their way to me.

Metro YMCA of the Oranges, YMCA of the USA Public Policy and Marketing departments, and South Mountain YMCA Executive Director Rick Gorab supported me during a pivotal time in my career. It was the opportunity that allowed me to pursue this writing.

I must thank the producer of *Why Should We Care about Child Care?*, Terry Randall, for discovering our center and sharing it so sensitively with the country.

The teaching and support staff of The South Mountain YMCA Child Care Center, who share their compassionate expertise with our children, their stories with me, and make my job so much easier. I am indebted to the leadership of my anchors: Kathleen Shaw, Julia Dixon, Alison McCord, Marie Papageorgis, Kathleen Jones, Marguerite McDougal, Jean Rysinski, Christine Jenkins, Tracy Reilly, and Jennifer MacAfee. And the devotion of additional long term staff: Marcie Kenney, Ellie Maziekien, Stephanie Riley, Kirbee Stern, April Pray, and Elain Lyons.

I am most appreciative to Dianne Matzner for providing me with such good query advice as I began this project. My agent Meredith Bernstein, shared her contagious level of spirited confidence in *Caring Parent's* right from the start.

The entire Prima Publishing team was graciously helpful, patient, and responsive to this author, throughout the entire process. Thank you for your guidance!

My parents Tanya and Charles Tabak gave me the warm gift of growing up with love and security. I am grateful for their unpaid publicist efforts on behalf of this book. It is without precedence! My sister, Karen

Honig, offered me insightful editing advice throughout my writing. I cherish our friendship.

My children became my partners, as my eldest daughter Andrea enthusiastically provided original illustrations, Traci made lists daily attempting to title the book, and Michael sat and reminisced his child care experiences with me. You are all my motivation and my treasures.

Last, but most, for my husband Frank. For doing double dish duty, extra homework help, twice the bed time stories, and more than your share of bath times. For camping in the wilderness, without a sleeping bag and with the bugs, and finding unique ways for me to have time alone to write. Your never ending encouragement, love, and support guided me to see this through to the end. You are my hero.

PREFACE

One of the parents from my center recently said, "We are being asked to do something our parents and their parents were never asked to do." I gave that statement much thought, since I counsel parents on a daily basis about their child care decisions. For most of us, when we were growing up, if Mom had a job outside the home, a grandparent or aunt living close by would take care of us. For a few dollars a week, a neighborhood teenager would take care of the kids during after-school hours. Socially, however, it was not considered favorable for parents to work and leave a child who was younger than school age in someone else's care. Only the financially well-off had live-in nannies. Nursery school became acceptable and a status symbol at that. At nursery school, children learned from educated professionals, two to three times a week for up to two and a half hours each time. Children were given a head start on their educations. These children then went to kindergarten prepared.

A child care center was an institution with minimal standards that cared for young children of less-educated working parents. The perception was that at child care centers, noses were wiped, diapers were changed, and crying, dirty children spent too many hours in an unstimulating, baby-sitting type of environment.

For the majority of us who grew up in the '60s, there was no quandary as to what kind of child care arrangement was best for our families. To think one might be spending the equivalent of a mortgage on child care costs, or to think that just six weeks after having entered parenthood one would be forced into the dilemma of separating from that new role for ten to twelve hours a day would have seemed absurd. Nevertheless, here we are, bringing in the new millennium, faced with these major decisions and more. Many of us are holding on to our careers longer and having children later in life. To survive in these economic times and raise a family, two incomes are usually required.

Staying home after the baby is born is no longer the rule, but is becoming more and more of the exception.

Families need to be supported in their choices, not chastised for them, whether they are staying home with their children, looking for in-home care, or searching for the right child care center. Today's parents need child care that is more accessible, more affordable, and more consistent with high-quality standards. Recent studies tell us that only one in seven (14 percent) child care centers is rated as good quality. The distance between quality and affordability is too great. Parents are forced to settle for programs that meet their financial criteria, but such programs may not necessarily meet high standards. The recent national attention and convening of the White House Conference on Child Care is a beginning step to the national awareness that is needed to address these issues.

—Elissa Tabak-Lombardo
www.caringparent.com

INTRODUCTION

In America today, there are more than thirteen million children in some form of child care. The single most important and anxiety-ridden decision every working parent needs to make is, "Who will care for my child?" Selecting the right situation, coming to terms with that decision, and surviving the reality of daily challenges are overwhelming responsibilities. As parents, we are desperate to make informed decisions about the care of our children.

A 1995 U.S. Department of Education Survey says 31 percent of children in child care are in center-based programs, and that percentage is rapidly growing. In preparation for the 1997 White House Conference on Child Care, Hillary Clinton said, "For too long, parents across our country have struggled with too little information, too few choices, and too much anxiety. It is now time to move this issue to the top of our country's agenda."

The aim of this book is to provide parents with that information, and to offer them peace of mind. Where other child care books cover many forms of care, this book is the only one of its kind to address the specific issues, joys, and obstacles of the child care *center*. It dares to present a child care center in its day-to-day existence, and to furnish parents with the resources they need to understand and succeed in it. An inside view of a child care center is revealed.

My goal is to give readers a comprehensive understanding of how and why center life works, and then provide them with the tools they need to make it work for them. As this country embarks upon a massive early childhood awareness campaign, parents will have greater access to quality centers. The child care *center* is the future of child care in our country today. In my daily interactions with parents, I find them craving practical guidance and resolve on issues like:

- Why is my two-year-old biting all the children?
- How do I separate in the morning?

- Will my child love her caregiver more than me?

- Can't I sneak out as long as my child seems happy?

- How should staff be supporting my child's difficulties?

- What can I do to be more involved in the center?

- Why shouldn't the toddler class have more toys on the shelf?

- Where does my child care tuition go?

- Tell me why she's using the potty at the center, but runs from it at home!

The many years I have spent counseling parents regarding their child care choices and experiences have made me acutely aware of parents' needs during these stressful times. In response to those needs, key dilemmas are identified and solutions for working through them step by step are presented, including:

- Finding a quality child care center

- Making the adjustment to a child care center setting

- Understanding life in a center

- Networking with other parents

- Parenting stress

- Surviving the reality of day-to-day challenges

Sharing some of the more poignant as well as humorous anecdotes from past years will help you identify with those who have walked in your shoes before.

For the over four million parents whose children are in child care centers and for the millions more who are soon to embark upon the child care center journey, this book aims to fill the information void. My hope is that this book will help you embrace and find knowledge, comfort, understanding, joy, and success in one of the most emotional issues you will ever face.

The Decision

Is a Child Care Center
the Right Choice for Me?

So you're past the agony stage of "Do I have to go back to work?" You have reconciled with the notion that we are entering a new millennium and you are not June Cleaver. You and your spouse have landed back on the ground after having had the passionate experience of becoming parents. Nobody could have prepared you for the feeling you had when they put that baby in your arms. You thought you would know. You knew it would be intense, but the magnitude of this passion was not one anybody could have accurately described to you.

It is time for reality to set in: for going back to work, and for deciding on child care arrangements. This is obviously a most important decision. However, if you wait until shortly before your return to work to decide on appropriate child care, you will find that your choices will be much more limited. This is not a decision that should be taken away from you, so that you find yourself settling for whatever arrangements are available. If you cannot go to work with peace of mind about where your child is and whom he or she is with, you will not be able to do your job. It's best if you can take time to prepare and do your homework several months prior to the time when you will need child care.

What Are My Options?

Because caring for a baby is such an emotional issue, there are many conflicting viewpoints on the subject.

Every family will have different needs and different comfort levels. What's right for one is not necessarily right for another. At the 1997 White House Conference on Child Care, Hillary Clinton summed it up when she said, "One-size-fits-all child care" just doesn't work. Parents need to find the situation that suits them best. Of course, where in the country you live will determine the availability of each of your choices. Your options will most likely fall into one of these categories:

- **In-home care:** care by one adult in your home (nanny, au pair, neighbor, relative)

- **Family care:** care in the home of another family (providing care for up to six children, may or may not be licensed)

- **Child care center:** a state-licensed facility caring for several groups of children of various ages

There are distinct pros and cons to each choice, and based on your own personal circumstances and requirements, you'll be able to determine which is the best one for you and your family. In-home care seemed to be the more popular choice during the '80s, when child care centers were getting a bad rap. The '90s seemed to have reversed that trend with au pair and nanny horror stories that have left even the most ardent of in-home care supporters thinking twice.

> It's best if you can take time to prepare and do your homework several months prior to the time when you will need child care.

The Pros and Cons

In-Home Care

There are some important pros:

- It is a very secure feeling to know that your child is in your own home, among her own things, and able to maintain her schedule with little, if any, disturbances.

- There is no fear of other children's germs making your child sick.

- There is the security that when your child does get sick, you can still go to work.

- Extended hours are usually not a problem if you need to leave very early, or return late in the evening.

- There's no need to drag your child out in inclement weather.

- There is no question as to who is caring for your child. There are no changing of shifts, lunch breaks, or other staff changes.

- There is also the added bonus of having a load of laundry done for you, beds made, and maybe even dinner started.

Take note of the con list:

- There are no checks and balances in place—who's watching the nanny?

- It can be unreliable—you're depending on one person to be always available.

- It is the most costly option for one child.

- The caregiver's personal needs, due to isolation, may not be met.

- There may be a lack of professional training on the part of the caregiver.

- There can often be language barriers, in the case of au pairs, between the parent and the caregiver.

- Turnover can be frequent.

- In-home care can be intrusive to everyone's private lives.

Though many families switch from "nanny" care to child care because of the child's socialization needs, I get my best stories from what I have termed my "nanny call of the day." Every day I receive at least one phone call from a parent in a panic about child care and their particular nanny story. Though each of these stories has been a true one, I tend to hear many of the same nanny stories over and over again.

They go something like this: The nanny has left, or is leaving, without notice; the nanny stole from them; the nanny is getting under their nerves; the nanny is in love with the child's father; the nanny hit the baby; the nanny is pregnant and didn't tell them; the nanny misses her family, boyfriend, or cousin, and must leave; the nanny ignores the baby and just talks on the phone all day watching game shows; the nanny stays out late every night; the nanny must leave to take care of a sick friend or relative; the older child does not like the nanny; the nanny didn't put the child in a car seat; the nanny had a nervous breakdown; the nanny's references were fabricated by the nanny agency; and the stories go on and on and on.

> Every family will have different needs and different comfort levels. What's right for one is not necessarily right for another.

One of the biggest problems with in-home care is the lack of checks and balances in place to ensure that quality care is being provided. Video surveillance cameras are becoming more and more popular for parents to check up. If abuse or neglect is detected by a surveillance system, though, it's after the fact—the child has already been hit, yelled at, or ignored. There can even be questions concerning benign neglect, like "Did the baby get her medicine?" The bottle doesn't look like there is any less than there was before you went to work, but the nanny says she gave it. Well maybe she did, maybe she didn't. The fact remains, that with no one to check up on all of the particulars, chances are you will never know.

There are also still the issues of the unreliability of the nanny and her personal needs. It can be very isolating being in a stranger's home with no family and friends, taking care of someone else's young child. Will this person be at her best taking care of my child under these circumstances? Though there are many wonderful and honest in-home care providers offering a much-needed service, the percentage for uncertainty and the unknown is high.

With in-home care, don't forget about the added burden of being an employer. Social Security and Medicare taxes need to be paid, and you need to apply for an employer identification number. Check with your tax advisor about all of the legalities.

When the in-home caregiver is a relative, there can be much peace of mind regarding the trust you have in that person. Make sure, however, that it's a relationship that can withstand some stress. Do you have the kind of connection with this person to be comfortable telling them you don't like the way they burp your child? To tell them, "No, my child is not malnourished, please feed him as I asked?" To disagree with them on the outerwear your child should be wearing when they take him for a walk that day? Clear the air up front, and set some ground rules. Children need the consistency of parents and caregivers who are of similar philosophy and practice. If you are tiptoeing around issues that are important to you and the care of your child, there is the strong chance you'll go nuts!

Family Care

The pros of family care:

- The small, cozy home environment and personal relationship that a family provider can offer is a most endearing quality.

- There are usually not more than six children in this person's care.

- Children will not get sick as often as they would in a child care center, but certainly more than if they are at home with one adult and no other children.

- There is the added benefit of the cost per child, which is usually less than in other child care settings.

Unfortunately, the pros of the family providers make a short list.

The cons of family care:

- Because there is such difficulty in states being able to monitor adherence to standards, many regulations and standards are not complied with.

- There are no checks and balances in nonregulated homes, and only occasional checks and balances in regulated ones.

- There are statistics that now tell us children in family care settings get hurt more often than those children in child care centers or those children at home with Mom. The dual roles that are played as in family provider settings and at home with Mom (taking care of baby, laundry, etc.) are distracting from the single role that caregivers have in a child care setting.

- Discipline and limit-setting issues may not be consistent with the parents' philosophy.

- The provider may be less professional with business matters.

- A parent needs to arrange for back-up care when the family provider gets ill or goes on vacation.

- There are fewer opportunities for the family provider to get ongoing training.

As with in-home care, the family provider is just one or two people, and there is little relief in the caretaking during the day. If children are of different ages, nap times will vary. That means the person caring for your child is most likely working eight to twelve hours daily without a break. Anyone who works with children knows this can be very taxing on the nerves.

Child Care Centers

The child care center has been the focus of much media attention recently, as our country embarks on an early childhood awareness campaign. The reason centers have received this attention is that they can set standards and follow up on their implementation. The pros of child care centers:

- Checks and balances are in place.

- States have the ability to set standards and requirements for centers and to grant licensing. Safety and cleanliness measures must be checked, and health records must be on file. Child to staff ratios must be maintained, as well as group size.

- There is a chain of command that is followed.

- There are educational requirements for all teaching staff.

- There are opportunities for training of staff on many levels.

- Children are engaged in programmed activities.

- Those in group care settings are more likely to have professionally trained caregivers.

- More than one caregiver is present at all times. This goes a long way in case of emergency situations and in protecting children from abuse.

- Only about 1 percent of all child care abuse cases originate in child care centers.

- Children have more choices among different toys, books, and puzzles.

- Interaction with other children and adults becomes very natural and comfortable for the child. Young children who have been in a positive group care setting have shown the ability to form warm and trusting relationships with other adults in addition to their parents. A child care center can be a small environment with as few as ten children, or a large one with several hundred!

The cons of child care centers:

- One of the biggest drawbacks of a child care center is that children get sick more often.

- You do need to have a back-up arrangement for that day when your child wakes up ill and you have an important presentation to make. It is an unfortunate fact of group care. Even with diligent hand washing and stringent cleaning of toys and surfaces, children will spread germs either by touch or by air. The close contact with other children guarantees some exchange of germs. The good news is that these children's immunities are built up at an earlier age, and as they get a little older, they do tend to get sick less often than their non-child care peers, who have not had similar exposure. Cautionary word: Children who display signs of chronic severe illness (febrile seizures, pneumonia) will find that exposure to other children in a group care setting will perpetuate these illnesses, and alternate care must be further explored. Always consult your physician if your child's health is a concern.

> Young children who have been in a positive group care setting have shown the ability to form warm and trusting relationships with other adults in addition to their parents.

- Your child may receive less individualized care. The quality of the center plays a major role in maximizing individualized care, maintaining and exceeding standards, and minimizing illness in a group setting.

As you do your research, you will discover there is good and bad represented in each of these child care options. Finding *high quality* makes the difference in reducing the *con* side in each of these settings. As licensing standards become more stringent and consistently followed, child care situations of all kinds will be improved, and our children will benefit.

Philosophy

The last component to making this most important decision is determining your own personal philosophy and making a good match with your child's caregiver. It is imperative that the person(s) who is taking care of your child not only respects your philosophies but shares them as well. A good center should foster not only the growth and development of children but also of their families. As a child grows, attention should be paid toward nurturing his social, physical, emotional, and intellectual development. Different children will progress at different levels in each of these areas. It is the responsibility of the adults caring for your child to be aware of his progress in each area of growth. Each child should be seen as an individual, not just a member of a group.

The needs that you have for your child make up a great deal of your philosophy.

- How much outdoor time do you want your child to have?

- How do you want your child disciplined?

- How do you deal with food issues?

- What limitations do you want your child to have?

- How do you want her tantrum handled?

- Is your crying child going to be held and nurtured?

- Will the caregiver interact positively and playfully with your baby daughter?

- Is she going to be supported in her play and curiosities?

- Is her individuality going to be respected and celebrated?

- Are her self-help skills going to be fostered and applauded?

- Will she be encouraged to make choices that are appropriate for her age?

- Is the environment rich with literacy and age-appropriate materials?

- Is the parent viewed as the first and most important teacher?

You may find yourself searching for your own answers to those questions.

Learn Through Play? Or Academics?

More often than not, a parent visiting a center will ask, "So, do they do any learning here?" Or, "At what age do you start to teach them?"

The early childhood years are filled with so many exciting opportunities for children's growth and development. These opportunities are supported when children are enticed in their curiosities, motivated in their play, and encouraged to make safe choices. I have often told parents, "We can teach a three-year-old to read, and a fifteen-month-old to use the toilet, but why would we want to?" Parents often get caught in a competitive rush for their child to succeed. There is no evidence of children who are taught to read at four years old (versus the average six years old) being more successful later in their school experiences. What is known, however, is that for children to be successful in academics later on, a good foundation needs to be laid in these early years. Children can be children only once, and they can't help but learn every day! The world around them, and how it relates to them, is their priority. If something is not in their world, it doesn't exist. By introducing inappropriate academics at too early an age, children can be turned off to the school environment later on. By not allowing children's natural interests to lead them, adults are imposing their own interests on children, and potentially losing them. Young children need to learn through play and rich experience, not ditto sheets, flash cards, *or* seat work. In later chapters, as we discuss developmentally appropriate practice (DAP) and how it relates to each of the age groups, we offer interpretations of the different kinds of play our children engage in.

Do you want your child in a program that encourages hands-on experiences? One that empowers children to make careful decisions and that practices a learning through play philosophy? Most definitely yes!

> It is imperative that the person(s) who is taking care of your child not only respects your philosophies but shares them as well.

2

The Search

Finding and Selecting the Right Center

By this time, you have received so much advice from family, neighbors, and friends that your head is swimming. You have desecrated every magazine you could find and cut out any article that offered checklists and hints on assessing your future child care center. You are organized and armed with notebook, pen, and an agenda of questions for this interrogation. Where do you start?

Your Personal Needs

Before you can consider any center, you must be aware of what your own needs really are. What are your requirements for a child care facility? Though a center may come highly recommended to you, if that center doesn't fit your lifestyle, it will not be a good match for you.

The Center's Location

The factor most important to a majority of parents will be a center's location. Proximity and convenience to home and work are prime considerations when making this decision. For some parents, child care close to work is a priority. When you're at work and receive that dreaded call from your child's caregiver telling you that the child is ill, it's reassuring to know you can be with your child in a short amount of time. The hardest ride home is one in which you are racing to get to a child who is not feeling well. Can you imagine how your anxiety would be heightened if that race were two cabs and an hour's train ride away?

Before you can consider any center, you must be aware of what your own needs really are.

Other benefits to child care that's located close to your workplace are the middle-of-the-day visits and lunches you can share with your child. You can look forward to a peaceful ride home together, which can provide some one-on-one time for you and your child. Depending on the length of the car, train, or bus trip, commuting together can work positively, or not, for you and your child.

Other parents will seek a child care center that's located between their place of employment and their home, hoping that they are increasing their options for choosing among centers. This *can* offer a greater range of possibilities, especially if choices near home and work are not the best. If your commute from your work is not too great, getting to your sick child won't cause too much distress. Not too surprisingly, many of the parents I've encountered over the years who have chosen their child care facility between home and work ended up moving nearer to the child care center after all! The social lure of the families with whom they had formed relationships through the center was a strong one.

The majority of parents I meet, however, do look for care close to home. The comfort and familiarity of neighborhood families who attend the same center, being able to sit on the train with other parents of your child's class, and having the support of others who can pick up your child when you are running late from work is more commonly available in your hometown. Because so many families move while their children are young, a neighborhood center greatly increases opportunities for meeting other families in the community. Many families will network together for carpooling, baby-sitting co-ops, and emergency care. Meetings in the park and established play dates are natural benefits of the relationships that evolve. The stress factor on those days when a child is sick is still fairly high, but for these parents it is outweighed by the many other comforts and advantages of their children already being close to home. Not all towns, though, will have centers that fill your needs and offer good care. It is imperative, then, that you weigh all contributing factors to this decision.

The Center's Cost

It doesn't seem quite fair that you need to even think about cost with a decision such as this one. We're talking about your child's health and safety! You want the best for your child and do not want to think that the price of that will be an influencing factor. Sadly, the gap between quality and affordability is still a large one. You naturally will gravitate to a center that has a good reputation and high standards. We know that these standards are defined by low child to teacher ratios, higher-salaried and better-qualified staff, and superior facilities. It comes down to plain math. Unless there are private grants or government subsidies, income to support the greater salaries, benefit expenses, and state-of-the-art equipment will come directly from the tuition you pay.

> Be realistic when determining the funds you have available for child care costs. You do not want to put yourself into a position of debt that will in the end compromise the consistency of care for your child.

Be realistic when determining the funds you have available for child care costs. You do not want to put yourself into a position of debt that will in the end compromise the consistency of care for your child.

Ask your employer if it participates in any programs that assist workers or subsidize child care costs. There are many different types of tax credits and pre-tax income deductions for child care expenses. Some of these programs are well-kept secrets and may be available through your employer. Many nonprofit agencies that operate licensed child care programs will offer scholarship assistance as well. You can

One of our single parents was having a difficult time managing the cost of the center. Cali would charge her tuition each month on a different credit card, and then pray. When she got too far in debt, as she did several times, she needed to pull her children out of the center and have in-home care. After months of inconsistencies and problems with providers in her home, she returned to the center, hoping something would change that would allow her to make it work. Cali needed to do this at least four times over a two-year span at our center.

approach organizations like local YMCAs, religious community centers, churches and synagogues, Boys' and Girls' Clubs, and hospital-based programs with inquiries about scholarship availability.

The Center's Hours of Operation

Finding a center that is open the hours you need may be challenging. Some parents' jobs require that they come early and stay late—others offer flexibility. Many parents have long commutes; some work out of their homes. A lot of families have found success by having one parent go to work early and come home early. The other parent leaves for work later and returns home later. This type of schedule has a few benefits. The parent who leaves for work later can bring the child into the center in the morning. That parent has some one-on-one time with the child, and there is less stress to get out of the house at the crack of dawn each morning. The other parent comes home earlier, keeping the child's day at the center a little shorter or accommodating an earlier closing time. The same time for togetherness and closeness with the child is now available to this parent at the end of the day.

Though it may be tempting to take advantage of centers with flexible and extended-day options, whenever possible, do so with caution. It is a prolonged and tiring day for a child who is dropped off as early as six or seven in the morning and then is not picked up until seven at night. Families that do not have strong support or are dependent on just one parent have more challenges to minimizing the time their child spends at the center. Some of these children spend twelve hours a day, five days a week in care, and need a break! Ideally, these extended hours are designed to accommodate parents whose workday starts earlier *or* ends later, but not both.

Size and Type of Center

Child care centers will range in size anywhere from as small as fifteen children to as large as several hundred children. Though most will fall somewhere in the middle, many parents will find comfort in one type of center versus another.

Some parents like the intimate ambiance of smaller centers, where there is a more casual and personal feeling to the operation. There is no business office to deal with or policies that need three committees to evaluate changes. The owner is usually onsite and may be your child's teacher. You can speak directly with the owner daily. Chances are, because of their smaller work forces, these centers will be open fewer hours than their larger counterparts, and will close more for holidays and snow days. They usually have more flexibility, though, when it comes to accommodating your individual needs.

A mid- to large-sized center might have a hustle-and-bustle atmosphere that lets you know things are moving! Like smaller centers, they may be private or public, part of a franchise or chain, and for- or not-for-profit organizations. Though they may not offer flexibility in policy and practice, these centers offer something else: additional staff and resources. With their greater personnel pool, you don't have to worry about staff making it in to open the center when an inch of snow has fallen or a storm is blasting through. There will also be a chain of command in place, and you can talk candidly to the director about a teacher without them being one and the same person. Many larger centers will also have access to parenting support, which may offer workshops, educational programs, and social events. Some centers can be so large, however, that the number of children in their classrooms may be higher than what you'd like.

Corporate child care centers are greatly increasing their percentage of the market. Many large (and some smaller) companies and hospitals have invested a lot of resources and funding to provide this benefit to their employees. Though corporate centers have the reputation of a more institutional feel, if you prefer a more formal atmosphere, you might be more comfortable in this setting. Usually parent support for the center is strong, but networking among families is less common because of the commuters and more transient parent body. Corporate centers are experiencing rapidly growing success, however, as professional child care companies are being hired to set up and run their operations, and employers are responding sensitively to their employees' needs.

Days the Center Is Closed

This one can really mess a family up. Some centers are open year-round. They will close for the six major holidays of the year, and no more. Snow days are a rarity, and you can always count on the center to be open for you. Other centers may follow the township's school calendar. Unless you work for the Board of Education, you can find yourself looking for care on each holiday, snow day, and vacation break. Not including the summer months, you may find yourself scrambling for child care on more than thirty days out of the year!

Though most centers will fall somewhere between the two extremes, this is a critical question to ask. The majority of facilities may be open for twelve months of the year, but expect that they will close for teacher in-service days and/or back-to-school spruce-up for a week or two at the end of August.

Center-Provided Meals

Some centers provide meals for the children, and some centers don't. You may be required to bring breakfast, lunch, and possibly snacks for your child. Though this will add to your preparation time, you will know what your child is eating and how it was prepared. Many families love it when centers provide a hot lunch for their children. This is only a benefit, however, if your child likes the foods on the menu, and if you approve of the menu choices as well. Then you get a break from preparing meals, and the peace of mind that your children are being given healthful meals. Some centers, though, will serve many foods high in sodium and fat—such as fish sticks, chicken nuggets, and french fries—as a routine diet. Your child may eat them, but at what price? Check out the menu, ask if fresh foods are prepared and cooked in their kitchen daily, or bulk ordered frozen and then heated. If you or your child do not approve of the selections, ask if you can bring your own. Some facilities may ask that you don't do this, afraid of a commotion among the children. Look to a center that honors and respects parents' rights to provide their children with meals as they see fit.

The Center's Flexibility

Do you work only part of the week? If so, do you have the option of adding an additional day to your child's schedule should your needs change? What about switching days? Are your part-week schedules set in stone, or is flexibility available to alter those days on a weekly, as-needed basis? How about for emergencies—is the center helpful to families in those instances? The more full-to-capacity your center operates, the less versatility it may have.

Drop-In or Emergency Care

Though some facilities will offer emergency backup care for families who have not registered at the center, you will more typically find this kind of care available through corporations that offer it to their employees. These programs will be available for a limited amount of time to families who may be between providers, or when schools are closed. If your center provides

Plan to take the day off to be with your sick child when the occasion arises. Take one large afghan, a pot of soup, a large box of tissues, and a plentiful pile of books. Add one under-the-weather child, with one overworked parent, and you have the perfect recipe for an excuse to do nothing but nurture and nuzzle your day away.

backup care to children who are not regularly at the center, ask how this may influence your child. Is there a different class roster every day? Or is drop-in care a separate class by itself?

Sick-Child Care

Just as you're waking up on the morning of an important meeting that you have organized, your three-year-old enters, announcing that he doesn't feel well. You take his temperature: 102 degrees. Every working parent's nightmare. Well almost. Some centers do have sick-child programs at their sites or an alliance with a hospital that provides this service. There will be guidelines for how sick your child can be, however, and some centers will not take children who have the usual contagious childhood diseases. Not all states permit sick rooms in a child care facility. This option can be a wonderful benefit; unfortunately there are not many of these programs.

If the center you are talking with has invested in this specialized care, find out how it works. Do children need to be registered in the child care program to take advantage of it? What are the costs? How sick can a child be? Is it for mildly ill children? You know, those with colds or recovering ear infections? Or will the center accept some of the more uncomfortable ailments like chicken pox, strep throat, bronchitis? Is there a maximum limit to the amount of days you can use this program?

Some progressive employers subscribe to programs that place nurse's aides who care for employees' sick children in their own homes. Depending on the policy, the employer may absorb costs partially, fully, or not at all.

When a center has a sick-child care option, it certainly is an attractive lure, though centers that do not have this benefit are not usually discounted.

Plan to take the day off to be with your sick child when the occasion arises. Take one large afghan, a pot of soup, a large box of tissues, and a plentiful pile of books. Add one under-the-weather child, with one overworked parent, and you have the perfect recipe for an excuse to do nothing but nurture and nuzzle your day away.

Parent Involvement with the Center

As working parents of young children, finding the time to be active participants in a center can be challenging at best. Find out what the center's expectations for parent involvement are, if any. A co-op program will naturally require more participation from parents. These co-operative centers require that at least one parent from the group volunteer in the class daily; they may also operate with a parent governing board. For the most part, however, a parent body will formally represent the families of the center, organize fund-raisers and events, and act as liaison to the administration. Your availability will determine whether you can honor the center's requests for commitment. Believe it or not, a center that does require parents to take some kind of active role is a gift in disguise. These centers offer you firsthand knowledge of and input to their operation and are typically more responsive to parents' needs.

Your Child's Needs

After location and affordability are considered, a large part of your decision will be based on your gut instinct and your personal compatibility with the administration.

She may not have told you in so many words, but you know this better than anybody. Will she fuss on a long car ride to child care, or will she enjoy the trip, making it a special time for the two of you? Maybe she will benefit from an extra half-hour sleep in the morning if you choose a center close to home. Then again, maybe she's ready to rock and roll by 7 A.M.! What about her anxiety with group interactions? Does she have a difficult adjustment in larger groups? Perhaps she thrives on the commotion. As you look around to see whether a center feels right to you, can you see your child's personality and needs fitting in to this setting? Though you will make your decision about child care as an adult, from an adult point of view, only you know your child well enough to include these considerations in your ultimate decision.

Resource and Referral Agencies

Finding child care programs to evaluate is getting much easier! Let your fingers do the initial walking, and call your county's child care Resource and Referral Agency (R&R). This agency in your community has several functions:

- To provide consumer education and information to parents regarding child care options in their community and some pertinent facts within those options;
- To assist with training and technical assistance and act as consultants to child care providers; they may also help centers meet licensing and other standards;
- To work with employers in helping them understand their employees' needs and offer programs to facilitate meeting those needs.

When you call the R&R, they will give you the names of centers that are located within your requested proximity. The R&R should have infor-

Assessing Individual Centers

Once you have assembled a list of centers to contact, take your time, take a pen and pad, and settle in. You will want to talk to the director on the phone to do your preliminary screening. When you make your calls, pay attention to how the phone is answered. Does the person sound friendly? Are there screaming children in the background and some adult yelling at them? If so, hang up and don't call back! Eventually you will reach a friendly voice that can offer you some real information. I had one parent tell me the reason she knew we were the right center was that I took time with her on the phone, answering her questions and validating her parental concerns. Other places she had called couldn't be bothered with her on the phone. She immediately felt un-

mation about the centers that will help you narrow down your search, such as ages of children accepted, hours of operation, tuition rates, accreditation status, meals provided, transportation availability, scholarships, and licensing capacity. These agencies receive consistent feedback from parents and licensing boards and should have a good handle on quality issues. Parents report to them when they have had positive and negative experiences with the centers the agency has referred. Some of these agencies, however, may not always be up to date with the most recent statistical information on a center (rates, hours open, wait lists, and availability). Ask when the information was last gathered.

Most communities will have a Resource and Referral agency for public access. If yours does not, the local community can assist! Ask your pediatrician, realtor, Welcome Wagon, neighboring community organizations, and the young families in the park on Sunday.

connected to these centers and uncomfortable about pursuing them. Comfort level is extremely important as you proceed in your search. As you do your preliminary phone interviews, identify the basic criteria that are important to you.

Compatibility with Administration, Philosophy, and Goals

There are so many facets to consider when you are making this choice. After location and affordability are considered, a large part of your decision will be based on your gut instinct and your personal compatibility with the administration. The administrator or director sets the tone for the center. The staff are hired, trained, and evaluated by management and take their cues from these people. The mood of the center will certainly be reflective of their influence.

Though there are several schools of thought in early childhood education, generally the philosophy of a center will fall under one of three main categories: academic learning programs, Montessori programs, and learning through play programs.

Academic Learning Programs

Academic learning programs focus on teacher-directed learning. We have already discussed that academic environments are inappropriate for young children. Though academic learning is not the nationally supported theory, many people still advocate for and support these programs. Academic learning programs promote children sitting in chairs for lengthy periods of time and following group standards. Such programs are often a result of pressure from parents who want their children to succeed in today's world, and from educators who are used to public school systems and apply school-age practices to children in early childhood. Parents want their children to advance and learn new skills. They inaccurately believe that these academic abilities are necessary early on.

The more parents educate themselves on the appropriateness of academic learning programs for young children, the less likelihood these programs will endure.

Come to your appointment prepared to ask questions and take notes.

Montessori Programs

Though this is a grossly oversimplified explanation, true Montessori programs reflect Maria Montessori's philosophy of multi-aged groups of children being taught through a prepared environment. Children are empowered to make choices throughout their day, and a learning through play philosophy is celebrated. These multi-sensory hands-on experiences reward young learners. By preparing the environment, manipulatives and such made of hard woods are introduced to the children. These pieces have only one correct way to be assembled or function. Children's goals

Clarice's and Peter's mom came into our center one afternoon, on the verge of tears. In an attempt to keep her two children at the same site and save some money, she investigated a new local child care center. She had Peter, her eighteen-month-old son, with her at the time.

"I asked the director what the philosophy on potty training was," she told us. "She looked at Peter and said, 'He should be in underwear.'

"'But he's only eighteen months,' I replied. She told me he was too big to be wearing diapers, and if he were at her center, he would be trained and in underwear. Not wanting to tackle that any further, and marveling at how the two- and three-year-old children were sitting at a table doing their seat work, I asked her how she would handle my three-year-old daughter, who didn't like to stay in a chair for long.

"'Oh she would follow the rules here, you don't have to worry. She'll stay in her seat.'

"'But what if she didn't?' I asked again.

"'But she will,' the director insisted.

"'But what if she won't?' I persisted.

"'Well then we would call you, and you would tell her that she needed to listen or you would be very angry with her and punish her.'

"That was the moment I picked up, and ran."

are to problem-solve the *right way* of using them. The idea is to give the child a task that is challenging but within the child's ability to accomplish successfully. Then the child's feelings of satisfaction and self-worth are heightened as the child is able to make it work. Some critics of these programs say the process is too structured, and that children experience failure at tasks and ultimately become discouraged.

The biggest problem with programs that claim to be Montessori schools is that not all of them truly are. Many centers attach the name to their operation without being true to the philosophy. By purchasing some of the formal Montessori equipment, they claim to practice the program. In fact, educators should be formally taught and trained in the highly regarded Montessori program. It is worth doing some homework on these programs, so that you can determine if the center you are interested in is a true Montessori center.

Learning Through Play Programs

Learning through play programs focus on child-directed, teacher-supported play, which practices developmentally appropriate practice (DAP). Practitioners of these programs also believe the environment plays an important role in facilitating children's play and imaginations. Children are enlightened through a hands-on approach to actively doing and embracing the relevant world around them. They are cooking, planting, and being challenged by an environment that is rich in language and expression. The multisensory approach to learning draws in their interest and implants the foundation for a love of learning. This philosophy is the most widely practiced of the three philosophies and is supported by the only national certificate program for group teachers—the Child Development Associate (CDA)—by higher education throughout our country, and by the National Association of the Education for the Young Children (NAEYC).

Tours

Take a day off from work. The only way to visit a center and meet with the director is to do so during the normal operating hours of the center. To try and squeeze this appointment in on your way to work, during the parents' drop-off time in the morning, or on your way home from work, during the pick-up time in the afternoon, is not a good idea. You do not want to make a decision about a center based on the

> Caleb's mom approached me one morning, after meeting a prospective parent in our parking lot. "She said she was on her way to work, and only had a few minutes. Her nanny left yesterday. She has never been here before, but remembered hearing good things about the center. She came to sign her two-year-old up to start tomorrow, if there was room." I don't understand why most people put more time and thought into shopping for a pair of shoes than shopping for a child care center.

most hectic times of the day. You want to see the center and its staff during *normal* operating hours—the hours typically not seen by working parents.

As you make your way through your tour, the center's appearance and aesthetics will be an important part of your decision making, but don't rule out the center that is not as dolled up as you would have liked to imagine. The newest intercom system, computers, or the fanciest carpet don't necessarily tell the story. Look for general signs of orderliness and cleanliness in the entrance area. Is there a parent board? See if there are upcoming meetings, active committees, parent notices, and communications posted. A center with strong parental involvement is much more likely to be family-friendly and responsive to the needs of their parents.

Interviews

Come to your appointment prepared to ask questions and take notes. As you meet with the director, find out general information about the center:

- How long has it been open?

- How long has the director been there?

- What is the relevant history of the center?

- How many children are they licensed for?

- How many children do they have?

- How many children are in each class?

- What are the teacher to child ratios?

- Is there flexibility for part-time children?

- Can schedules be changed, or are they firm? Is there an open-door policy—meaning parents can come and visit at any time of the day?

- Can anyone come and pick up your child?

- How do you arrange for someone other than yourself or your spouse to pick up your child?

- What measures of security are in place to ensure that only authorized people can pick up your child?

Answers to these questions will assist you in narrowing your search and enable you to evaluate centers with confidence.

However you decide to proceed with your search, it is worth the additional pains and inconveniences of your time and consideration. This investment will pay off as you reap the benefits of peace of mind while you are working.

3

The Evaluation

How Do They Measure Up?

The centers you've found are all located conveniently and are as affordable as you are going to get. Now that you have selected several centers that meet your basic and most fundamental requirements, you are well on your way to comparing them, and judging their overall quality. Because of the broad distinction between standards represented in child care, finding the superior centers can become confusing and frustrating. Take along some patience and a clear head as you proceed.

Chances are, if you were to visit ten centers, you would see ten variations in the quality of care provided. You will undoubtedly come across those centers that do what they must in order to get by, but not enough to ensure high-quality standards. Lack of adequate funding may be responsible, with resulting low salaries for staff, inadequate space, and meager materials. Such centers will certainly stand apart from those with enough qualified teachers and superior facilities. Making an assessment among the centers will become easier the more you do your research.

Accreditation

Since 1985, The National Academy of Early Childhood Programs (a division of NAEYC) has coordinated a voluntary accreditation system. The overall goal was, and still is, to improve practices and reflect high quality in child care programs. The Academy awards accreditation to programs that successfully complete a three-step process that can take from six months to two years. Accreditation specifies standards and criteria that professionals in the industry have determined represent highly effective programs. This process is initiated by an in-depth self-study that takes a child care center on a journey through their program, examining practices, philosophy, and facility. After modifications are made to improve the program as a result of that self-study, an on-site visit is made by professionals who validate whether or not those changes have been accomplished and quality standards maintained. A commission then makes the final decision on acceptance for accreditation. Though it is a time-consuming and painstaking undertaking, once validated, this accreditation signals to you that the center maintains high standards for early childhood care. This award is valid for three years.

> If I had to give just one criterion for a novice parent to look for when evaluating a center . . . I can't help but answer instinctively, "The happiness of the staff and the children in the center."

I would not interpret this accreditation as automatic acceptance of a center or rejection of those that do not have it. There are centers that may have accreditation but are not a good match for your family's personal needs. Many centers maintain exceptional standards for quality care without having gone through the accreditation process. Organizations like the YMCA or corporate and franchise child care companies may have their own accreditation systems. Most, however, will use the NAEYC criteria as their foundation. It is certainly a reliable sign of quality if a center has this prestigious accreditation. As you seek out child care, following the sign of an accredited center will be a great starting point. Be aware, though, not to substitute your own evaluations and personal satisfaction goals for this symbol.

What to Look for When Visiting

Those initial impressions count when you are walking into a center for the first time. A center that pays attention to details in one area is likely to pay attention to details in most. The person who greets you as you enter the building, whether it's a front desk receptionist or a caregiver going by the entrance, conveys much about the program. What is that person's mood? Is she pleasant and courteous, or not too happy to have had to answer the door? Can he assist you or does he not know where to turn? So much is conveyed when a staff member passes by you with eyes cast down at the floor, versus a welcoming, "Hi, how are you?" When you receive a friendly smile, a doting look at your new baby, or an invitation for your visiting child to join the group in session and have snacks with the children, you are going to feel *welcome.* That's one of the goals of your search and evaluation!

I have often been asked, if I had to give just one criterion for a novice parent to look for when evaluating a center . . . I can't help but answer instinctively, "The happiness of the staff and the children in the center." Contented children and staff truly are the product of a quality care program. If children were not being attended to, from their most basic needs to their most peripheral ones, their mood would reflect of it. To attain levels of happiness the children must be:

- Physically comfortable (fed, well-rested, clean, and wearing a dry diaper, in a safe environment)

- Emotionally secure (receiving plenty of attention, can anticipate environment with the help of caring adults, and responded to with warmth, nurturing, and positive direction)

- Intellectually challenged (played with, engaged in conversation regularly, read to, involved in appropriate activities, enveloped in an interesting environment, and not overstimulated)

In order for staff to give as much of themselves as quality child care intrinsically demands, their needs must also be met. Staff must be trained to provide surroundings that support health, safety, and developmentally appropriate practice, and they need to be provided with adequate space and furnishings to implement that knowledge. As professionals, they must be financially compensated and treated in a professional manner.

I encourage parents to approach staff, even on a first tour, and talk to them. "How do you handle children when they cry? What do you do about aggressive children in the setting? When do you have the time to communicate with the parents?" Answers to questions like these acquaints you with the teacher's style and allows you to determine if his or her response is in sync with what you believe it should be. It's also OK to ask how long they have been at the center, and even if they are happy there.

> While walking around the center, listen to the noises around you. Are they pleasant? Is the environment filled with happy sounds?

While walking around the center, listen to the noises around you. Are they pleasant? Is the environment filled with happy sounds? Is the music loud and blaring? (We hope only in the room where the children are dancing.) Are there many babies crying at one time (as may easily be a result of the domino effect)? If so, is each baby being taken care of in loving arms? Is the crying short-lived? Are awake babies confined in cribs, swings, and playpens, or playfully engaged and being tended to? What about the staff's voices—are they loud and angry with the children? Do they call from across the room to them? Are the children fighting a lot, so that the teachers appear to be doing too much refereeing in the class? Whose voices do you hear most? Is it the teacher giving instruction, direction, and discipline? (Let's hope not!) Preferably you're listening to the children's happy voices—busy, chattering, and occupied in their learning environment—the babies gurgling and playful, with their caregivers and teachers calmly supporting those roles.

Another telltale sign along your stroll through the center is the fragrance in the center. Granted, when you are near the baby or toddler area, the fresh change of a diaper or the recent creation of a freshly soiled one will have a potent and slightly lingering scent around it. However, that scent should not permeate through the facility, nor should it linger in the room of offense for very long. Dirty-diaper garbage should be contained in cans with covers and removed from the center all through the day. You may be aware of a light disinfectant in the air, or nothing at all. A stale dirty-diaper odor not quickly alleviated can be a red flag to pay close attention to the rest of the hygiene practice in the center.

The Facility: Cleanliness, Health, and Safety

Though we may be forgiving of our own less-than-perfect adherence to immaculateness at home, we should not tolerate anything else in our child care center. The exchange of germs in a center results in children and adults getting sick. We expect some of that, and try and prepare for it as best we can. The more illness occurring in a center, however, the less likely that the center is following strict guidelines for cleanliness and health. The best prevention against illness in a group setting is still the simplest: washing hands. Ask the questions, "When do staff wash their hands? When do children wash their hands?" The response to both should be: "Frequently. Before and after all meals and snacks, after diapering a child, after personal bathroom use, after wiping a nose or cleaning spit-up, and after cleaning a table or any other surface in the center." These answers should be in addition to the obvious ones, such as after a messy art project or outdoor play. Children's hand washing should be included in those instances at all times, including the babies! Though not required everywhere, I always look for staff to be wearing gloves during soiled diaper changes and food serving *in addition to* the hand washing. As you tour the center, look for soap dispensers in each bathroom and kitchen area. Visually follow a staff member after they diaper a child or wipe a nose. Do they head directly for the soap and water?

Babies and toddlers love to put things in their mouths. Every toy or book within a hand's reach will end up there. How do the adults at this center handle this? Expect a system to be in place for washing and sanitizing toys on a daily and weekly rotation. Once a toy has landed in a child's mouth, there should be a caring adult nearby, prepared to take that toy upon surrender before it gets into the hands of another baby. A similar toy may be available and nearby if the toddler is then looking for it. These soiled toys, rattles, or books can be placed in a basket or container of some kind, stay out of reach and sight of the children, and wait for the daily cleansing of toys. Surfaces in the rooms should be wiped down daily with disinfectant, or weekly, in older-age classes.

Ask how often bathroom surfaces are cleaned (which should be very regularly) and how the general cleaning of the center is taken care of. Is there a service that comes in daily or weekly? Is the staff responsible for the entire center's cleaning? (This can be most taxing on teachers and caregivers.) How often are the rugs shampooed? Especially in baby and toddler rooms, where so much of their time spent is on the floor, it should be monthly, or minimally at least every two months. I do know of centers that shampoo their rugs weekly to minimize the spread of germs. Many centers also require all adults and visitors to wear disposable booties upon entering the baby room. This can minimize dirt on the floor surface from coming in contact with the babies.

I am often surprised how few parents ask what emergency procedures are in place at the center. Though no one, not parent, staff, or administration, wants to imagine a crisis on any level, it does rate high on the parent worry scale. Confront your worries, and ask the question up front. "Can you describe your procedures for emergency to me? Is there a chain of command? How many of your staff are certified in CPR and first aid? How often do you train staff in safety guidelines? Where is the first aid box stored? What kinds of accidents have happened at the center? Can strangers access the building?" Though these kinds of incidents are rare, we need to know there is a plan in place for dealing with them.

Continue your journey around the center. Think like a small child might. Look at the room from his eye level.

- Are there security covers on every outlet?

- Do you see smoke alarms and fire extinguishers?

- Are those sharp corners on the cabinets padded?

- How are the surfaces next to the indoor climbing equipment prepared? Do you see cushions or mats around them?

- Are children unable to leave a room without a staff member seeing them?

- Are chemicals and medicines stored up high, away from the children's reach, or in locked cabinets?

- Are children's bathrooms free from any locks on the doors?

- Is access restricted to kitchens? Do the cabinets and doors have child safety latches?

- Can only adults reach teachers' scissors, pens, and supplies that are stored?

The answer should be "Yes" to each of these questions.

Out of natural concern for their own children, parents have occasionally asked me if we had any children with AIDS in our program. This is a most delicate subject, which can dismantle one's confidence in the ability to provide for their child's safety. If the director does have knowledge of a child in the center with such a disease, the law prevents him or her from disclosing it. That confidentiality cannot be violated. Trust that licensing is not about to put *any* child at health risk.

Your state will require every licensed center to maintain a health record on file for each child and staff member. This will include all immunizations for babies, which need to be continually monitored and updated. Your physician should note any special circumstances, such as regular medication that needs to be administered, or allergies, on this report.

Health department regulations on immunizations and safety requirements for facility will vary from state to state. Local townships will audit these records, as will state licensing. You should not have to concern yourself over these issues.

On to the playground. Most accidents occur here, and many are a result of poor or inappropriate equipment, and/or negligent staff. For starters, is there a fence around the yard? Supervision is very difficult when there are no real boundaries. Then look at the surface surrounding the equipment in the area. Not all states require a protective surface, but it has been proven to prevent injuries from falls. There are many approved energy-absorbing surfaces, including:

- Wood chips (not my personal favorite because of all the splintering and naturally quick dissipation of the material. At proper depths though, they are considered adequate).
- Shredded tire (children get dirty initially after the installation, but that does not last. They unfortunately love to sample the pieces in their mouth. This surface, at proper depths, has good drainage).
- Rubber interlocking tile (good drainage and useable for tricycle riding as well).
- Sand (an old but safe subsurface to use. At proper depths it provides good protection, not great drainage however, and is an attraction to neighborhood cats).

If this center operates its playground on all blacktop, concrete, or dirt, without any cushioned surface, I would imagine there would be no climbing equipment and no running around. That doesn't sound like much fun to me.

Look over the playground equipment. Is it old and made of wood? If so, you will probably discover many opportunities for tender skin to be pierced with the splinters. Wherever you see metal equipment, watch out for danger from burning heat or freezing cold contacting the children.

- Do you notice any unprotected concrete?
- How about protruding screws or bolts where jackets and hoods can get hooked and pose choking hazards?
- Does the equipment look appropriately scaled to the age of the children using it?

- For the number of children expected to use the facility, does there appear to be enough running and play space?

- Do babies have separate outdoor space or equipment from the preschool children?

- Is there a cover for the sandbox to protect against visiting feline neighbors in the evenings?

I would suggest visiting the center while the children are playing outside. With the best of playground equipment and protection, if the adults are not attentive to those in their care, accidents will occur with more frequency. Look to see if teachers are congregating in one spot, using this time to talk to each other and take a break. I hope not! The presence of these people on the playground is not only to provide for the children's safety, but to continue the children's learning experience through rich play outdoors.

Accidents unfortunately will happen, and children will get their share of bumps and scrapes. As parents, we watch as our own children fall and get bruised right in front of us. Unfortunately, we know we are unable to prevent these childhood maladies altogether, but we can screen out those programs that do not minimize risks.

Licensing requirements provide for health and safety standards to be in place and maintained in a center. The day-to-day existence and continued implementation of them, though, may not be. These requirements vary from state to state, but unless there are current allegations against a center, or licensing is up for renewal, it is possible that state inspectors may not visit a particular child care center for one, two, or even three years! The more you know what to look for, the better equipped you will be when you make the decision about your own child care center.

The Staff: Background Checks and Procedures

Even though less than 1½ percent of sexual abuse against children stem from child care centers, this is still a natural worry of parents. Media hype heightens our worries, but such concerns are better confronted and disposed of than tucked away, still gnawing at us somewhere. Does the center allow a staff member to be alone with a child at any time? When the center opens at seven in the morning, even if only one child is present for that first half-hour, is more than one staff member present? The answer to that should always be "Yes." Even in cases where there is no threat of any abuse, we worry about emergencies and proper response to them. How can one person administer CPR and call for help at the same time?

What are the screening procedures for hiring new staff? Though criminal background checks do offer some security, they do not provide for full disclosure of an individual's criminal history. States do not have the ability to share these records, and few do federal criminal checks because of the high cost and lengthy turnaround time. Many states now require child abuse report information on every child care worker. These reveal whether any child abuse-related calls or claims have been made against an individual. A person may not have a criminal record, but if the Department of Human Services in your state has been called in on a domestic issue pertaining to a child, it will end up in this file. Determine that previous employment checks have been made, in addition to the formal background checks.

Is there a written procedure for reporting any suspected cases of abuse? Does the staff receive training in this sensitive but critical topic? What are the procedures for releasing a child to someone other than their parents? Several times a year either a staff member or I invariably end up sending home a very angry grandparent whom we are refusing to allow to pick up their grandchild. They hadn't brought any identification, and we had never met them before. You want to ensure that the center requires proper ID before releasing a child to anyone, even if the child calls the person Grandpa!

Ratios and Group Size

The quality of care provided to children is directly linked to the group size and adult to child ratios. Not surprisingly, these specific factors also impact directly on the cost of that care. The more staff, the higher the expense. The fewer number of children in a group, the lower the center's revenue. The direct link to quality and cost is easily traced, and then passed down to you, the parents, through the tuition.

Between these two quality factors, if you're faced having to choose between a center with smaller group sizes and another with higher (but still acceptable) adult to child ratios, choose the one with smaller group size. When children are classed in smaller groups, the adults interact more frequently with them. They get to know the children and their parents more intimately and provide more individualized care. The environment also becomes a more peaceful one with fewer aggressive behavior problems. Though ratios do impact the quality of care provided (the more adults to children the better), there are good arguments for providing fewer caregivers, but more highly trained, educated, and professional ones. Imagine a room full of adults who do not have the skills, training, presence, or desire to work with babies. They do not talk to the babies, play with them, or follow standards. Having many adults in this baby room is worthless. Where there are highly trained, nurturing, educated, and motivated caregivers in a similar room, two adults with eight babies are able to do the job four adults at that other center could not do with the same eight babies, and they will do it much better!

State requirements for minimum ratios and group sizes vary greatly. In Massachusetts, centers are required to maintain a one to three ratio with infants nine months old. In Idaho, those same children can be in a ratio of one caregiver for every six babies! Group sizes show similar discrepancies. In Missouri, maximum group size for nine-month-old babies is eight, and in New Jersey, it's twenty! (See state by state requirements in chapter 12.) Child care professionals and experts (including the NAEYC) agree on the following standards:

- Babies, newborn up to one-year-old, should have a ratio of one caregiver for every three babies, with group size up to nine;

- Toddlers, thirteen to twenty-four months, should maintain a one to four ratio, with group size up to twelve;

- Toddlers two to three years old should have between a one to five and one to six ratio, with group size between ten and fifteen;

- Children three and four should maintain a one to eight or nine ratio with group sizes not exceeding eighteen;

- Children four and five should keep between one to eight and one to ten in their ratios, and should not exceed group sizes of twenty.

While you are visiting a center, you will get a sense of the staffing issues and how they relate to ratio and group sizes. What you will also discover is how the difference among centers boils down to the people you are now observing and getting to know.

More on the Center's Staff

What Makes a Quality Staff?

The stylist who cuts your hair every two months needs to maintain a license, but the adult who applies for work with young children does not. Much has been written about the lack of qualifications required for employment in the child care field in this country. As the new millennium approaches, and child care issues stay on the front platform, certifications and continuing education will be part of a package to improve that current situation.

Professional Qualifications

You certainly want to ask the director what qualifications she requires of her staff, from lead teachers to support staff. It is not unusual to find the director holding all of the state requirements for a lead teacher. Then those caregivers who are actually in the classroom on a daily basis are considered to be under her direct supervision. They may actually have no formal background in child care or with children at all. However they are the responsible adults in the room with these children. Expect that those teachers, teachers' assistants, and caregivers will all have different job descriptions and different requirements for being hired and for maintaining their positions.

With strong, consistent training in place, it is not necessary for each adult in the class to possess a college degree in early childhood education. Mixing of staff backgrounds in a setting provides for a healthy balance of knowledge and wisdom. Imagine a center filled with intelligent degreed young adults recently out of college. Or another run by wonderful nurturing moms. The energetic, youth-oriented, college-degreed group has current philosophy and techniques fresh at their fingertips, but is void of years of experience as well as the passions of a parent. Similarly, the seasoned maturity of the professionals that have raised children, know child development firsthand and have a greater understanding of a parent's perspective, but may be missing the impartiality and knowledge of the fundamentals of philosophy and practice of educating young children. With ongoing education and training enthusiastically received as a part of the continuance for each of them, the by-product of a healthy pairing of backgrounds is a well-rounded, child-sensitive, and appropriate environment. An ideal situation of mature, energetic, experienced, and degreed professionals is unfortunately rare, and in fact is an unrealistic goal in a field where financial compensation is minimal.

The Child Development Associate degree (CDA) is the only nationally recognized training and certification program for child care staff. It is a one-year program, which often originates from a college or community agency, and educates qualified individuals working in the child care field on appropriate standards of practice in child care. Many centers are seeking teachers who have this credential.

Ask the director how new staff members are trained and oriented. Find out what early childhood training is regularly incorporated into the program for teachers and caregivers. Two distinct benefits result from child care staff participating in these kinds of workshops. The obvious is the acquired knowledge about caring for and teaching young children. Less apparent, but just as invaluable, is the professionalism with which staff are treated. This recognition results in added commitment to their positions.

Personal Qualifications

Naturally, you want to ensure that state guidelines are being met (in some states exceeded), and that your child's teachers are receiving many opportunities for continued learning in the field. There are however, traits to look for in teachers and caregivers that fall outside the parameters of a tangible characteristic such as a certificate. It is the relationship between children and those adults who care for them that rates highest when determining quality. Look for these characteristics in caregivers and teachers:

- All staff should be affectionate, warm, and loving. Families are greeted upon arrival by name; babies should be held and cuddled; preschoolers are welcome to receive a hug.

The more you know what to look for, the better equipped you will be when you make the decision about your own child care center.

- These adults enjoy the children and their families; they get much satisfaction from spending time with them and are able to form attachments. Their respect for the family supports the parent-child relationship.

- Caregivers and teachers recognize children's feelings; they are sensitive to the children's needs and respond to them appropriately. Children are validated by such acknowledgment.

- Patiently listening to and *hearing* children comes naturally.

- The adults in this setting know how to set limits without being punitive. The discipline is supportive and strives to minimize conflicts.

- Quality child care staff know how to provide excellent physical care to those in their charge.

- Teachers are flexible, not rigid, in their routines or plans. It is their sensitivity to the children's needs that affords them the freedom and security to be spontaneous.

This relationship is critical to quality experiences for children in child care. They learn about themselves and others, and develop their love for learning.

Staff and Child Interaction

Not surprisingly, the best experiences for children, staff, and those watching on the sidelines happen during interaction. When the adults are engaged with the children, one-to-one and in small groups, the frequent contact between them results in high quality and valuable learning.

Many parents believe that if a structured activity with staff is not engaging their children throughout the day, they are not getting their money's worth! A high quality interpersonal relationship is not limited to a planned curriculum. In fact, it is the simple daily routines of diapering, hand washing, meal preparation, or the common experiences together of watching the rain fall or a bulldozer move a pile of dirt out the window that provide opportunities for this relationship to grow. Adults who take advantage of everyday teachable moments like these by talking with the children about them, or listening and expounding on the children's thoughts are doing many things:

- Encouraging language development

- Providing opportunities for rationalizing

- Deepening the connection between the two

- Offering trust

- Saying, "You are fun to be with!"

It is amazing how children will take the value of these relationships and bring it with them to others! When a child is new to our center from another child care arrangement, I always want to know about the relationships that had been in place previously. Whether it was with a nanny, baby-sitter, or another child care center, was it a positive one? Or one that contained much anxiety and apprehension? My experience has been that when children come to us from solid, trusting, and confident caregiving situations, they are far more likely to transfer that trust and enter their new arrangement with us positively. By contrast, those who had former relationships that were more troublesome or had experienced many caregivers in a short amount of time tend to cling more and have transitions that are more difficult.

How are these staff members relating to the children? Are they comfortable being playful? Not all adults are. It takes a very special adult who is able to sit on the floor, be silly, tell stories, build block towers, lend an ear intently trying to decipher this foreign language, squish her fingers through the finger paint with the children, and laugh! These collective groups of people whom you are watching—teachers, assistants, and caregivers—are the ones with the capability of ensuring your child's success, growth, and happiness in this environment.

Staff Turnover

The neighborhood supermarket offers twice the benefits; working at the corner drugstore has less stress; the waitress at the local franchise is treated with more respect; the sales clerk at the mall has better opportunity for advancement; and guess what? Though these jobs require less formal education, they all pay more than teachers and caregivers receive in the average child care center. One of the biggest dilemmas in child care is finding and securing qualified staff. Because of the horrendous pay scale and lack of professional advancement opportunities, this is typically a high-turnover occupation. We already know one of the most important factors in a child's success and happiness in child care is directly related to having consistent care from qualified, nurturing professionals. The quality of interaction between caregiver and child is the proven strongest link to quality care.

How can a center provide for this kind of care when turnover is high? They cannot. Children are unable to depend on the stability of an environment when there is a revolving door of faces and personalities to greet them each day.

What is the typical number of child care employees the center maintains? Determine the center's turnover by asking them how many teachers and caregivers left the center that year. An average staff retention rate of around 60 percent annually (the national average) is considered poor. When four of every ten teachers/caregivers are leaving their positions each year, the programs continuity will be lacking. Quality is a direct result of this. If a center claims a lower than typical turnover, find out why. Chances are most likely that the staff is:

- Being recruited from professional backgrounds with formal and practical experience as a requirement,

- Better financially compensated than the industry average,

- Receiving health insurance, sick days, retirement, and vacation benefits as part of their employment agreement,

- Composed of mostly full-time employees.

It is time to worry when most of the adults employed at a center do not work regular and full-time hours weekly. Many centers seek to keep their employees working fragmented hours for several reasons:

- Flexibility to extend hours when needed without worrying about overtime,

- No benefits to pay,

- Lower salary requirements,

- Larger staff pool to pull from when someone is out sick.

This doesn't work for the following reasons:

- There is less cohesion among staff. There are always new people coming and going, fewer long-term employees.

- Parents and children rarely get to know staff and develop relationships. There are just not enough hours in a week.

- Employees are not there to "hang their hats," so there is rarely ownership of the program among staff. Those all-out efforts may not be made.

- When personnel are so poorly financially compensated, it reduces their morale.

Children pick up on the moods of the adults caring for them. When spirits are low, the smallest children are the ones who will feel it. Odds are strong that these people will not stay for long if they are not happy, for any of the mentioned reasons.

The adults caring for your child need to provide all the things you have been looking for; they also need to be well-trained, have a strong background rich in experiences, and understand child development. Rarely does an employer invest much into training for those who are working the least number of hours. As the turnover slows, and retention increases, so does the level of care your special one receives.

Developmentally Appropriate Practice

You have probably seen the term *developmentally appropriate practice*, or *DAP* splattered all over every article, book, and handout relating to child care you have gotten your hands on. You might define these words together to mean: "The manner in which growth is responded to properly." That kind of sums it up!

The National Association for the Education of Young Children (NAEYC) has published guidelines to educate parents, teachers, and governments which illustrate how young children between the ages of 0 and 8 learn best, and the best ways to teach them. When these guidelines are applied properly, they will contain two main objectives: to be 1) individually and 2) chronologically appropriate for each child.

We all know how each of our children has their own unique characteristics—physically, intellectually, culturally, emotionally, and socially—that separate them from others. When the adults caring for them provide experiences and interactions that are sensitive to that individuality in conjunction with their knowledge of how children develop, that practice is said to be *developmentally appropriate*.

Each of the age groupings in the early childhood years (0–8) will specify different standards of practice and suitable methods for implementing them. The common denominators that cross over all of them are:

- A supportive and nurturing environment where caring adults
  in the room respond to each child's own individual needs, and

- The provision for the methods in which children learn most
  effectively.

That formula tells us that children understand their environment best by doing. The style is language rich, and an integrated play-oriented one that is hands-on with concrete objects, not formal or academic. A good curriculum makes sense of all of the many real experiences the children have, and allows them to initiate the direction the learning takes. They need to do things for themselves! Adults provide guidance rather than instruction, which has proven to be of little or no value to children during these young years.

Chapter 6, "The Survival," and chapter 7, "The Endurance," illustrate how developmentally appropriate practice is related to infants, toddlers, and preschool children specifically. When a *child-initiated and teacher-supported approach in play* is used toward learning, it is meaningful. It is also one of the most important pieces of developmentally appropriate practice.

Siblings at the Center

One of the comforts we can find when leaving our children at a center or school is the knowledge that their brother or sister is just a classroom or two away. A program that is sensitive to the needs of each family will be responsive to times when children will benefit by the presence of each other. Some centers will not want to chance disruption of a child's adjustment or allow mixed-age groupings to participate together. When you are placing two children, or adding your new baby to your preschool child's program, check with the administration and teachers as to their philosophy and practice on this.

One of our toddlers, Alan, was having a difficult adjustment to his new baby brother's presence in the home. When baby Alexander joined the center, Alan was adamant that Alexander not enter *his* classroom. Mom abided by his wishes and brought the baby to the nursery first, and then Alan to his class. After the first week or so, Alan requested a visit to the nursery to see his brother. The staff happily obliged, and made a very special time for them. As days continued, so did frequent visitations. Alan got used to having a brother (as much as any toddler can) and mom shared with us that Alan came home full of tales about *baby Alexander*.

Another sibling team had their own routine. Every afternoon the toddlers and preschool children would be out on the playground together. When time came for the children to come inside the school, five-year-old Gail would join two-year-old sister Elizabeth's class. She participated with the toddler children during their afternoon *circle time*. Both girls would giggle together savoring their snack, and mothering instincts surfaced as Gail would read stories to small groups of toddlers, while her sister cuddled on her lap.

In addition to strengthening individual family ties, the combining of age groups has many wonderful benefits. Older children's nurturing traits appear as they take care of and watch out for younger children. They love to feel as if they are teaching and guiding their smaller counterparts. Self-esteem is peaked during these experiences. Younger children also profit, as they look up to older ones and wishfully mimic their advanced language and skills, thereby honing their own.

Although you may not have to find care for more than one child at a time, how a center responds to those individual parent needs may tell you much about the center's *view of the family* during your evaluation.

The Family-Sensitive Center

There may be volumes written about finding quality child care centers. Few, though, discuss the value of the relationship between families and their centers. Your children are spending many hours in the care of others. If that care is not reflective and respectful of a household's cultural and personal individuality, it can undermine rather than enhance the effectiveness of that family.

Look for a center that seeks to work together with parents, focusing on agreed-upon goals for the children. A center where parents are al-

Part of me feels like I am sharing in their day, when I hear Alan tell me these stories. Knowing they each have a piece of their family right there with them has eased some of my own guilt pangs.

ways welcome and made to feel at home. Where communication is not a chore on behalf of the staff, but the means of enlightenment and discovery in the children's best interests. The aim for consistency between home and center is achieved through a mutually respected and continuing dialogue. This center provides opportunities for parents to contribute significantly to their child's day, knowing their preferences are highly regarded and that the ultimate decision making about their children is in their hands.

From simple requests like, "I want my baby to sleep on his side," "Wake my three-year-old after only forty-five minutes of napping," and "Please keep a bib on my son all day because of his excessive drooling" to the more complex requests like, "Our family's religion does not celebrate birthdays; please do not include my child in celebrations of other's cupcakes and candles," "Let my four-month-old cry for at least fifteen minutes before you pick him up," "Keep my five-year-old out of the sandbox. She has very difficult hair to get the sand out of." And, "Don't hold the bottle for my nine-month-old, I want him to start doing it himself." Parents' wishes must be respected and validated, and unless harm is believed to come to a child as a result, ultimately followed. Ask the center under consideration how they would respond to some of those requests. Where rigidity and policy is offered as a defense for not being able to accommodate parents, you may still have some searching to do.

Often though, a conflict of philosophy may be at question. Through shared knowledge of child development and agreed-upon compromises, however, families and centers can work situations out before deciding that there's been a mismatch. Other times, that mismatch is best determined as soon as possible. "Don't let my three-year-old son play in any of that dress up stuff—that's for girls," "Please send homework home with my four-year-old; she refuses to practice writing her words with me," "Tell my son you will call me if he continues to act up—I'll straighten him out," "Don't let my three-year-old son use pink marker again—that's for sissies." These were all requests from parents that our center denied over the years. After explaining our philosophy on the various issues, we ultimately felt we could not honor those parents' requests, and there was no room for compromise.

Families come to us in all different packages, and with a little creativity, centers can be sensitive to their needs in a variety of ways. Some things our staff have done to try and help the families in their care have been:

> If you're faced with having to choose between a center with smaller group sizes and another with higher (but still acceptable) adult to child ratios, choose the one with smaller group size.

- A three- and a four-year-old just adopted from Russia into the same American family joined our center. The staff went out and purchased a Russian-English dictionary to facilitate communication and make the children feel more comfortable. As a result, all of the children in the class learned some Russian words!

- A South American child just two years old was new to our center and our country. Though the staff for her age group and class was not bilingual, another one of our teachers was, and made a point of visiting her each day. She spoke to the child daily in her native tongue, engaging her in conversation.

- Just a few parents over the years have requested staff use only cloth diapers on their child. Though caregivers find it simpler to use disposable diapers, all were happy to accommodate these parents.

- Several parents were rushing each morning to catch their trains. By slightly adjusting our hours of operation and opening the center just fifteen minutes earlier, we were able to give them time for breakfast with their children and catch the earlier train without a fuss.

- Several children of same-sex parents motivated us to acknowledge the void in our literature and include such families in traditional story telling.

- Parents of a speech-delayed child in therapy trained the staff to do language exercises each day to assist the child's progression.

Though these are just one center's answers to some of the needs their families have had, every community and family will discover their own. Can you think of a way your center might respond to your own family?

Recommendations from Other Parents

If you forget anything—or everything—else, don't overlook asking for references from parents in the center. This is common practice, and the director should have several to many parents who are happy to give references for the program. A great sign is parents who have been with the center for a while. Ask to speak with families that have children in your child's age group as well as other age groups. When you are *buying* a center, the aim of most is to stay in the program for a longer span than their child's current age group. You need to know how your toddler will fare when he becomes preschool age. Staff has been known to move around the center as well. You want to verify the consistency to the quality of the people who will be with your child all day. Are the adults in the class as highly regarded in the older groups as they are in the one you are placing your child in? What about the baby room? You've been thinking . . . there's a possibility next year. . . .

Talking to other parents with children in the center will tell you substantially more than either the director or teachers can. Even if you have had a recommendation to the center prior to your going there, it's

Anthony's mom shared her experience with me:

"We waited a long time to have Anthony. I planned everything down to the letter. My exact date to go on maternity leave, how long I would be out, time to shop for child care, and then eventually returning to work after six weeks at home with my new baby. I worked very long and hard to attain my advanced status with my employer and had never considered any other options. I was determined to prove being a mother would not change my performance or dedication to the firm.

When the time came to investigate child care centers, I was still optimistic and methodical in my plans. I made all the calls in advance, and set up appointments with the few that seemed to meet most of my criteria. As I rode up the long driveway to the center, I didn't know why I started to tremble. As I picked Anthony up out of his car seat, a sinking feeling came over me. I composed myself as I placed him in the Snugli and proceeded into the building.

The director made me feel wonderful. She was warm and compassionate, and seemed to really care about the families. I was feeling much better. After talking for about fifteen minutes, she offered me a tour of the baby room. Anthony quietly slept curled up on my chest. We approached as the sounds of classical music playing softly beckoned us in. The room was bright and cheerful. Cribs were in a sleeping area adjacent to the main part, and were not in clear view. Large windows with

reassuring to have a conversation with another parent. Once you have made your own personal visit and started to assemble your thoughts and opinions, you will find yourself with a different set of questions than you did previously; other parents can answer them.

- How long has your family been in the center?

- What are your overall feelings about the care your child has received?

hanging plants gave the place a cozy feel. Carpeted risers hugged the perimeter of the room, and cushions and low shelving units sectioned off the room into smaller, more intimate areas. There, in the middle of all of this, were several caregivers playing with the babies on the floor. One caregiver was engaged in a game of peek-a-boo with three other babies. Two other babies insisted on climbing up and down the carpeted risers over and over again, as the adult looked on with affection. Another caregiver sat in a nook with three babies, one in her arms having a bottle, the other two content to dump buckets of toys, as they motioned for their caregiver to keep refilling it.

What a lovely sight. Each of the babies was obviously being well cared for and was happy. Just what I was looking for. Wasn't it? I started to get teary-eyed. Then I began to sob, uncontrollably, and had to bolt from the room. I met up with the director in the parking lot. "The babies seemed so happy," I wailed. "I don't know why I'm doing this—but I can't do this—I can't leave him. How am I going to leave him?"

Anthony's mom had never considered not going back to work, until that moment. She went home and agonized with her husband over the unexpected feelings that were consuming her. After much deliberation, anxiety, realization, and a commitment to a lifestyle change—and to the envy of the other new parents she knew—Anthony's mom resigned from her job to be a stay-at-home mom.

- I noticed the toddler teacher seemed kind of young. She appeared good with the kids, but how is she in communicating with the parents?

- The director said there is flexibility in changing days. Have you had this experience to know if that is really true?

- What difficulties have you had with the center? (Assume that there have been some issues, and let them tell you, "None.")

- What is the best experience you have had with the center?

- Do the children get hurt often?

- Is your child happy?

How does this person sound? Listen for sincerity and credibility. Does the parent appear proud of the program?

Go back to the Resource and Referral Agency you called during your search. See if the agency can put you in contact with other families they referred to this center that are enrolled as well. Doing this might provide a less-biased point of view than a family hand-picked by the director. Your R&R and state licensing board will have any complaints logged against the program as well.

Hearing answers to questions like these from another parent's voice will furnish you with a different perspective of your evaluation.

Trust Your Gut!

Even in uncharted territory, you are your own best judge. After the referrals and after the visits, some things will just stand out to you, without explanation. It can be the voice on the phone, the handshake of the director, or the noise level of the room. Or it could be none of those. You may not know what or why it is, but it is. Your gut instinct goes beyond the tangible excuses to run from a center, and past your temporary parental hesitations of leaving your child. It can also tell you several things:

- I'm not comfortable—I need a more formal/casual atmosphere.

- I don't like these people—I can't relate to them; they can't relate to me!

- I need more time.

- It doesn't feel safe/clean/happy/sincere/caring.

- The environment is cold and impersonal.

- Get me out of here!

or

- Look how happy these children are!

- The teachers really seem to care about the kids.

- There is a warm and loving feeling here.

- These people are just like me. They understand what I am going through.

- Why did I wait so long?

- This is what I am looking for.

Staying at Home

In rare cases, your gut feeling can also surprise you.

Staying at home has become a luxury that, even with a lifestyle change, few new parents can afford. In addition, the majority of the families I meet consider staying home for as long as possible, and wish that the inevitable weren't. The pain of going back to work and leaving your child is a real one. As new working parents, we become consumed with insecurities. These doubts find us continually reassessing the choices we make. With a lot of support and compassion, though, most parents make the adjustment successfully and will integrate their new lives very positively with their old ones.

At risk of criticism, however, I must add that there are those parents who need to find a way to be at home. The anguish that they suffer through in the attempt to do it all may undo all they are trying to achieve. In the end, parents need to be true to themselves to make child care and going back to work, work!

4

The Transition

How You and Your Child Can Make the Adjustment

A parent of an eight-month-old, new to child care, described her experience as "mourning" for the loss of her child's innocence. She had been home with her daughter up until now. Her baby was no longer going to be the center of the universe for those taking care of her. She now had to "compete" for attention, toys, and space. This mom had accepted the reality of her need to return to work but had not yet forgiven herself. Another mom described herself as "courageous" for dealing with the inevitable and proceeding with leaving her newborn son as she resumed her career. Still another mom told me she kept praying something would change that would allow her to stay home with her child.

For babies—newborn to ten or twelve months—and their parents, this is usually the most emotional of transitions, as they deal with numerous issues at this difficult time. There are so many sentiments that a parent experiences during this period. A tremendous sense of guilt can be overwhelming for some, while panic and anxiety can affect others. If sadness and a sense of loss are experienced, it can be very difficult to resume "normalcy." Whatever emotions you are experiencing, one of the most important steps to a successful transition is support. Support from your family, from those you are close with, and then from the center.

I remember one mom telling me she was tired of defending her choice to return to work and enroll her child in a child care program to her friends. Having to explain your choices and defend your actions to family and friends adds more anxiety to an already agonizing experience. Interrogations from well-meaning grandparents can also undermine your security.

Parent Kathy Carliner from our center was once asked, "How can you leave a four-month-old in a child care center?" She said she thought about it for a while, and then realized, "You can leave your child—and you can go to work—only when you know that the person who takes him out of your arms every morning will not only take good care of him . . . but will enrich him . . . will love him . . . and will keep him very, very safe from harm."

Wow.

I thought this statement summed up our common goals as parents and child care providers. What more could we ask for?

To reach these goals, the center must understand and validate your needs by accommodating them and working with you toward a positive experience. Whether your baby is three months or three years, as a parent you should never feel as if you are leaving your child with strangers in a strange place. The only way to accomplish this is through time and good communication. Though as a parent you do not always have the luxury of a lot of time to introduce yourself and your child to the center, it is worth using up some vacation or sick time to ease both of you into this new situation. By gradually increasing the amount of time you spend at the center during the transition period, you provide answers to unasked questions. You establish relationships with caregivers that you would otherwise not have an opportunity to establish, and you participate in a part of the day you typically would not see! Parents' worst fears are arrested.

> Whatever emotions you are experiencing, one of the most important steps to a successful transition is support. Support from your family, from those you are close with, and then from the center.

Babies and Toddlers

For babies and toddlers, I suggest a minimum of three to five visitations over a two-week period of time. Arrange your first transitional visit with the center director. Ask her what the best time is for you to arrive. You do not want to be there when other parents are dropping their children off. The staff will need to focus on these parents as they go about their daily transition with them. You also do not want to arrive at lunchtime, otherwise known in our center as "happy hour." Staff will need to be 100 percent focused on the children in their care and will not be able to give you the attention you need at this time. In the baby room, usually by ten o'clock in the morning, several babies will be napping, and staff will be available for you to get to know. The younger your baby, newborn to five or six months, the easier time he will have adjusting to this situation and to his new caregivers.

Toddlers should be in a circle time or activity by 9:30 to 10:00 A.M. This is a wonderful time to settle in with the routine of the class and get comfortable. A song, finger-play, or a short story in a circle while you and your child sit and participate together is nonthreatening for both of you.

Your child may display one of the following two extremes in his conduct during these transitional visitations, but most likely behavior will be somewhere in the middle.

1. Your child may be very clingy to you, not wanting to leave your side (most typical of ten- to twenty-four-month-old transition, or a child who may have had a negative experience prior). If your child is hanging on your side, become an active participant in the class routine. (Even if that means he is on your lap) By singing along with the class, playing at the water table, welcoming the other

> You can leave your child—and you can go to work—only when you know that the person who takes him out of your arms every morning will not only take good care of him . . . but will enrich him . . . will love him . . . and will keep him very, very safe from harm.

children around you, or just intently listening to the story, you are modeling a desirable behavior. Do not be concerned if your child does not seek to interact with other children. Interactive play at this age is not natural. Your goals at this point are to make your child comfortable in the surroundings, get to know the staff and the routines, and think of this new environment as a place to have a good time. Do not sit in a corner from afar and watch the children with your child on your lap. He then has no motivation to become comfortable with this new group. As your child displays anxiety in the new surroundings, keep reassuring him that you are there with him, and try and interest him in something in the room.

2. Your child is off and running. He may appear not to notice your presence, but don't be fooled! If your child explores farther and farther away from your side, you can sit back and watch, or participate with the other children in the class. He will probably take breaks every five or ten minutes to check up on you. Give him a hug and a smile, and tell him how great he is doing and how much fun you are having.

You will be able to determine the length of time you spend at each visit by your child's ease of adjustment. Typically, a parent and child in transition should gradually increase their visitation time at the center. Then decrease your time, and increase your child's time without you.

The First Visit

On your first visit,

- Don't stay more than an hour.
- Get comfortable with your baby without deviating from his normal routine.
- Sit on the floor with the other babies and staff.
- Play with the other children and your baby.
- Ask questions as they occur to you.

- Watch the staff interact with the children.

- Get to know their routine.

- Become acquainted with the staff as you talk about activities, the routines, and the center.

- If your infant is mobile, let him crawl around.

- Allow the staff to get to know him. If he resists them, there is no need to push. Time will aid the process.

Your baby will *read* and follow your cues. Your tension and comfort level will be his. Also remember, while the parent is present, a child won't truly "bond"' with another adult. This process will happen when the parent is not present, and the baby comes to rely on his primary caregiver. By enjoying the children with your child and conversing with the caregivers, you will be getting a feel for the staff and how to approach them. Ask some of the questions that have been going through your mind that may not be covered in the center's literature. A confident staff will offer as much information as they can. Remember, the more you know, the easier their job will be!

Questions to Ask of Caregivers

- How many changes of clothing should you send?

- How long will the staff attempt to give a bottle?

- How do they heat the bottles?

- Do you or the staff set up the crib each week?

- How do they handle fussy babies? (Yours, of course, will not be one of them!)

- Who will be your baby's primary caregiver?

- Who fills in when that person is out?

- How many diapers do they normally keep on hand?

What most parents are not aware of is that the staff feel tension during these parental visits. A good staff person is very aware of the natural anxiety each parent is going through. They also know that they are under scrutiny. Their goal is to make you comfortable and trusting of them. Try to keep this visitation as nonthreatening to both of you as possible. This visit is the icebreaker.

Leisurely Visits

After your first visit, plan to make other regular visits to the center. Plan to set up the baby's crib, fill the changing table with your diapers and wipes, and set up your "baskets" of extra food, formula, clothing, and any personal items that you will be bringing to the center. Start to make it feel like home. You and your baby should be greeted warmly, and your presence in the room will be less obvious. Staff should be operating as usual. Participate in the staff's and children's play with your child.

By the third visit, you may consider leaving the baby for a short *trial run.* I always suggest that parents take an hour and do something for themselves. It could be getting a hair cut, buying new clothes for going back to work, or just a run around the block. It may feel like the longest hour of your life, but you are fulfilling some very important steps in the transition process.

1. You are giving your baby practice and a frame of reference of you saying good-bye, leaving for a short period of time, and then seeing that you really do return, in this new setting.

2. You are initiating the new trust between parent, baby, and caregiver.

One of our moms told me she sat in her car for the entire hour and cried. Her heart was pounding until she was able to get back to her twelve-week-old son. When she did return, he was most obviously happy and content. Though she knew she still had much work to do on this transition, she felt she had taken the first important step to their success.

Depending on how many days you have to make this transition, gradually increase the amount of time you leave your baby at the center. Keep your routine the same, but stay away a little longer each time.

Though you may have difficulty staying focused on any tasks while away from baby, it is easier doing this at home or running errands than trying to be at work and focused on your job. Don't be embarrassed to call and check on your baby, no matter how frequently you need to do this. As the parent, you have important answers and insight for the staff, who are just getting to know your baby. Caregivers are used to parent's concerns and calls and should welcome them.

The Ultimate Visit

Now that you have come this far, you may be ready to participate in the most challenging times of day at the center: Drop-off and pick-up times. It is worth the extra effort to come to the center at these times prior to your returning to work, so you can see and understand some of the madness without being frightened away.

Drop-Off Time

Arrive at a time that will coincide with the typical hours you will be arriving at the center when you return to work. Every parent is in a rush, and every caregiver is trying to transition a baby. Several parents may be giving instructions to caregivers at the same time. Some babies may cry as they react to the increased noise levels, additional adults in the room, and transition. Bottles are being put in the refrigerator, outerwear is being hung, supplies are being replenished, and cribs are being made. Some parents will have time to spend before leaving for work, and could be giving their babies breakfast or just playing with them as part of their daily transition. You may be wondering if this is the same center you have been visiting the past several weeks. If you haven't run yet, that's a great sign!

Each child will react differently to their parents leaving them. Many may not appear to care. Some may cry. It is not unusual for one crying baby to set off the alarm and for several others to join in. What is most important about being at the center at this time is carefully watching how the staff is interacting with and responding to the children. Are they assisting parents in their transition and good-byes? When the parents leave, are they soothing and distracting an upset baby? Are the babies engaged and happy in a short amount of time after the parents leave? Though chaotic in nature, this time of day tells a lot about the nurturing talents and organization of the staff.

Pick-Up Time

I always named the hours between four o'clock and six o'clock in the evening the *bewitching* hours for my own children. They've put in their day; they are tired, hungry, and ready for a calming change of pace. They are not sure, though, what they really want. This is the most difficult time of day for a child.

It is not unusual for children to spend an average of eight to twelve hours daily at the center. At the end of the day, each parent that walks in the room could be theirs! The children need a great deal of distraction and attention at this time. When the parents do arrive, it triggers the relief of their children's emotions. It is natural for young children and babies to cry when Mom or Dad enters the room. As with drop-off times, higher noise levels and additional adults in the room, added to the late time of the day, cause increased anxiety in the babies. It is important again to note the responsiveness of the staff. As parents approach caregivers, do you sense a warm trusting relationship? Are the caregivers sharing and exchanging information with the parents? In the best of circumstances, the drop-off and pick-up times of day are challenging. With warm and caring staff in place, you and your child will be well taken care of.

Back to Work

On days like this one, you know your head and your heart must not be connected. You did your homework. You did your research and found the perfect center to fill your family's needs. The environment is clean and cheerful. Caregivers are warm and caring, and the children are engaged and happy. You have spent much more time making this transition than any other new parent you know. So why is your heart so heavy?

For every parent it's something different. Anticipation of missing your baby's company, the thought of baby's smile upon waking, or the thought of someone other than yourself comforting your distressed

Y ou have done all the right things, said all the right words. You have followed the routine to the letter. You are trying to turn your child over to his primary caregiver, but your child is clinging to you for dear life, screaming and crying for you to stay.

baby. Maybe none or maybe all of these. Whatever it is for you personally, it is real, and it takes time to get past the sadness. Indulge yourself by calling the center frequently, and maybe sneaking out of work half an hour early.

Saying Good-Bye

I have been known to run out to the parking lot and bring back into the center a parent who thought sneaking out when their child was distracted was the best way to leave for the day. In the parent's mind, it was. They did not have to bear the pain of their child crying, nobody had to pry their child out of their arms screaming, and they didn't lose time getting to work as their child stalled their good-byes. What they didn't realize was that once their child looked up from their play and realized Mom or Dad wasn't there, the child started to cry. Then the child started to look for the parent. As a caregiver tried to calm the child, telling him "Mom or Dad had to leave, let's wave good-bye at the window," the child may have gotten more hysterical and difficult to soothe.

Regardless of your child's age, from infancy on up, saying good-bye is signaling to your child what will happen next. It is allowing him to anticipate the change and prepare for it. Even if your baby cries when you give him to his caregiver, you are saying good-bye, and that you will be back for him soon. Don't be afraid to ask the caregiver to take your child to the window or doorway to wave. Your child then has the visual reference of you leaving. When you return at the end of every day, you are adding the visual reference of Mom and Dad always picking him up. Knowing what to anticipate builds trust and security for your child.

As much as it hurts, you need to leave. I have had the unfortunate experience too many times of being asked to help pry a two-year-old's arm off of Mom, and into his primary caregiver's, so she could get to work. You need to turn your back and walk out. Hang outside the building or classroom if you need to, until you hear he has settled down, but do not let your child see you.

This extreme behavior should not last for more than two weeks. If it does, you, the director, and caregivers will need to communicate about additional strategies that might assist your child's progress. Some suggestions:

- Give your *almost*-verbal child the words he can't articulate: "You don't want Mommy to leave you today. You are sad and want me to take you with me." Though it may seem obvious in your mind that these are his thoughts, verbalizing them can confirm to him that you understand why he is sad.

- Give your child something with your scent on it, like a handkerchief, to keep as a reminder that you will be back for him soon.

- Have your child keep a picture of you with him.

- Toddlers love choices. Decide what choices you can offer him, like where he wants to say his good-bye to you.

- Have your child choose and bring a special book to share with his caregiver for when you say good-bye.

Allow enough time each morning to establish a transition routine. When saying good-bye, remind your child that you love him and will return for him at the end of the day. Then leave. Don't give mixed signals by extending or hesitating your departure. If you are feeling uneasy about your child's separation that morning, sneak in a back door and peek in the class. Make sure, though, that your child does not see you. Or, call the center when you arrive at work to see that he is OK. Your child's caregivers or the director may even call you to let you know your child is doing well.

There was one little boy, Jaimie, just two years old, whose grandmother used to drop him off several mornings weekly. At least once a week, Jaimie would cry so intensely when she tried to leave that he would make himself throw up. Though staff tried to assist, Grandma wouldn't leave Jaimie at the center. She would then take him home, and he got to spend the day with her. One morning, as Grandma was getting ready to take Jaimie home, I was able to convince her that we would clean him up and take very good care of him. After all, he wasn't sick, he just needed to know that Grandma needed to go to work, and we were there to help. Making himself throw up was no longer a reason to get to go home. We helped Jaimie get cleaned up, and he joined his friends in the toddler class. We told him Grandma needed to go to work, and we gave him a lot of TLC. Jaimie never made himself throw up again.

Waddling Toddlers

As babies approach that one-year-old benchmark, separation is difficult in the best of circumstances. A child who happily went from relative to relative at a family reunion, all of a sudden has changed his mind and won't leave your side. Children of these ages will probably need a longer time making the transition. Offer more frequent visits, and understand that your child will most likely cry when you leave him.

Initiate a routine with your child's primary caregiver, where you spend a small amount of time transitioning in the mornings—have breakfast at the center with your child, read a special story, whatever works for you! Then hand your child over to his caregiver (make sure you have designated a back-up caregiver on days when your child's primary is out), say your good-byes, and leave. After the first two weeks, chances are your child is distracted and engaged without tears before you reach your car.

The Fourth Day Wake-Up Call

A very distressed dad came into my office at eight o'clock one morning, and shut the door. "Something must have happened," he insisted. "My daughter enjoyed coming these past three mornings, but today she threw a fit, crying, refusing to come. I couldn't get her dressed, and getting her out of the car just now was horrific!"

I spoke with each of the teachers in his daughter's class to see if anything unusual might have taken place. As I had suspected, all reports came back negative.

Somewhere between the third and fourth day, reality sets in. The child begins to realize that *this is for real! We're going to do this every day!* It seemed fun and grown-up the first few days, but now the child is experiencing doubt and uncertainty. Separation anxiety is heightened.

Once you realize this is part of your child's separation process, you and the center can help your child adjust to his new situation.

- Have some photos of your family in your child's cubby or pocket. How reassuring to see Mom and Dad, even through tears. For pre-language children, this helps them communicate as well. Our center always keeps pictures of all of our children's families hanging around the classrooms, at the children's eye level. It is very comforting, even for a nontransitioning child, to go over and *share* his family with other children.

- Give him a special item from home that reminds him of family members. It could be anything from a scarf to a storybook. Try not to make it too cumbersome. As your child's security increases, his needs for these objects will decrease.

- Come visit the school playground on the weekend; your child will take pride in it being *her school,* and enjoy sharing it with you.

- Ask for your child to *borrow* a book from the class library. He will take delight the next day in returning it.

- Find out what special song the children sang or story the class read. Sing that song or read that story at home with your child. You are making a positive connection for her between home and school. Isn't it wonderful to see the recognition in her face when she realizes you know her *school* song?

Most important, have faith! Every child's needs are different, and there is no one solution. By remaining loving and positive but firm with your child, you will help him make this important transition.

Letting Go—Just Enough

Often, when the parent is having difficulty letting go, she may unintentionally compromise her child's ability to be successful at this new challenge. Some of the ways a parent might send this message are by:

- Asking for her child's permission to leave: "Can I go to work now?"

- Undermining the teacher's authority in the classroom: "Mommy's here, it's OK for you to climb on the table."

- Reentering the classroom after you have already left, upon hearing your baby cry.

- Bribing your child into letting you leave: "If you stop crying now and let Daddy leave, I'll bring you home a surprise today."

- Having a negative attitude in the classroom. I remember one parent's first day of school after seeing her child's name was

As babies approach that one-year-old benchmark, separation is difficult in the best of circumstances. A child who happily went from relative to relative at a family reunion, all of a sudden has changed his mind and won't leave your side.

misspelled on her cubby sarcastically exclaimed, "Oh great! What else is going to happen?" Naturally, her child began to cry, and the parent took it to mean her three-year-old was upset about the misspelled name.

As parents, being able to let go is not something we feel we should be doing with our young children. The parent that spoke about *being in mourning* for her baby's *loss of innocence* captured the emotions of many new parents. So how do we allow ourselves to feel better about a situation we still are not sure we subscribe to? There are no easy answers. If you have been fortunate to find excellent caregivers at your center, they will be understanding and compassionate about your feelings. If you are less assured about your parenting skills, they will graciously offer some helpful hints. If you are a seasoned veteran, they will sense your security and not interfere.

Preschool Children

If this is your child's first care out of home, you may be feeling exhilarated in anticipation of the new experiences she will have. The majority of children today participate in some kind of child care program. Most children with stay-at-home moms are enrolled for a part-day or part-week schedule. As a working parent, your child is spending longer hours in the program. Unless your preschool child has had a negative experience in another child care setting, transitioning should not typically include the drama that is part of an eighteen-month-old's separation from his parents. Plan on two visits the week prior to starting the program. Spend an hour or two during the *morning* meeting times and activity hours. Let your child venture out and explore while you remain in the background. Maintain a positive and cheerful attitude. If your child needs your assurance as she proceeds, freely offer it.

Be consistent with your morning drop-off routine, and let your child know what to expect. If you have the flexibility of keeping her first few days shorter than your usual workday, I highly encourage it. Adjusting to the new schedule will be easier if it can be more gradually introduced.

If your child has had a previous negative experience with a caregiver or in a child care environment, you may want to take additional time in making the change. Inform her new caregivers of the difficulties in the past. Make them partners in the transition.

Though going from a negative to a positive child care situation may be difficult for one child as she transfers those negative feelings, another child may leap at the new positive environment and not look back. It's anybody's guess to predict which your child will do. Most parents know their children well enough to give some helpful information to the teachers and caregivers. Don't hesitate to offer it. Maintain good communication about your child's daily progress. Spend time with your child each evening, sharing some of the highlights of her day.

How Children Adapt to New Child Care Arrangements

It's a rare instance in which a child has not been able to adjust successfully to his new child care arrangement. A smooth transition is the result of good communication, consistency between parents and caregivers, and sensitivity to the children's needs.

Babies

When a young baby is separated from her parents, she will be sad. She is experiencing a loss she cannot verbalize or communicate. Until she is comfortable in her new environment and has bonded with a caregiver, her sadness may be expressed through one or more of these behaviors:

- Not eating
- Not sleeping
- Being fussy

Fortunately, young babies tend to bond easily with trusted adults. Your baby should be back to her routine within one week after you have begun child care. Communicate with baby's caregivers as to what works best at home, whether it's swaddling, pacing, or rocking a fussy baby. Maybe the arm that you hold baby in for his bottle, is the reverse for the caregiver. If baby's regular habits are not back after a week, you should consult with your physician.

Toddlers and Preschool Children

At these ages, children may express their anxiety through a variety of behaviors:

- Tantrum throwing
- Toilet-training regression
- Anger
- Physical aggression
- Nightmares
- Changes in eating habits

Your child may exhibit these behaviors for several weeks. They should slowly dissipate as more time is spent at the center. However, at no time should you allow aggressive or tantrum behaviors to persist because of your guilt about leaving him. Encourage your child to use words to express his feelings. If he has not yet acquired the verbal skills needed, try and respond by acknowledging his anger (over whatever it may *appear* to be at that moment) but not tolerating the actions: "I know you are upset that you cannot take the ball home with you, but you may not throw it at me. You hurt me when you did that."

If your child is suffering with nightmares, just remain a comforting strength for him. Reassure him you are there for him, and always will be no matter what. Chances are he will not be able to tell you, or you won't be able to understand, what the nightmare is about.

When a child regresses in their toilet habits, it's best not to make a fuss over it. Treat the accidents as matter of fact, and have your child assist in the clean up. Your child might feel humiliated enough on his own. Don't make it harder on him by bringing too much attention to it.

Any changes in eating habits will probably correct themselves shortly. However, the emotional and nutritional needs of toddler and preschool children are unique. They may appear ravenous one day and barely seem to touch an ounce of food the next. Unless your child appears ill, trust his instincts. When he is hungry, he will eat. If you provide healthy food options for children they will have no alternative but to make wise choices.

As in all behavior that is unique for your child, remember to share it with your child's caregivers consistently.

Temperaments Count

Your child's own temperament—his own individual behavior style—will be unique to him, and will require different caregiving approaches. How an individual caregiver responds to his needs on emotional, physical, and intellectual levels will help determine the progress he is making in his transition day to day. As the person who knows your child best, you can help caregivers by offering information about him. Some children will respond to a quiet gentle approach, while others may prefer the distraction of fun music. Whichever approach works best with your child's temperament, communicating honestly with the people who will care for him is your best insurance for his success and happiness.

Parents Help Parents

One of the greatest assets to parents who are new to a center are other parents. Though the staff and administration may offer comforting words and suggestions, the other parents in the center truly can empathize with you and share your thoughts. Introducing yourself to other people is not as strained as it used to be. It's so much easier to talk to other parents when you are each holding a child! Participating in the same child care program, having children of similar ages, and dealing with comparable issues creates a bond that often results in wonderful friendships! Many of the parents at our center meet on the train or bus into work, at pick-up or drop-off times, or at social functions through the school. They have become a wonderful resource and support for each other. Seeking these parents out may provide the additional assistance you need to successfully work through your transition.

5

The Reality

Life in a Child Care Center

The Administration

Large or small, or somewhere in between; private or public; for-profit or not-for-profit. Whatever the type of center, there will be an individual or group of individuals who will represent the center's organizational structure on matters such as decision making, management strategies, and policy setting. The makeup of the center's administration may be as simple as a husband and wife partnership or as complicated as an early childhood professional who answers to supervisors, who in turn report to a branch board of directors, who then are accountable to a larger association board of directors! If there is a bureaucracy in place, the director of the center will serve as the liaison. Though a complex structure of hierarchy is less personal to a program, it also can work to ensure the stability, support, and continuity of the program in many ways.

The Director

Who is the director, and what is his or her role? The backgrounds of the leaders of your program can be varied. States' criteria for a child care center director are not consistent regarding formal educational requirements and actual experience. You may be evaluating a center where the owner serves as the director, and has no actual educational or administrative experience! The hiring of a head teacher to ensure programming quality and stability might fill any licensing requirements for that center. Another center's director may have successfully taught young children in a public or private school, and advanced himself to this new role. Though he is knowledgeable of appropriate practice with young children, this person's limited exposure and experience to the administrative tasks and leadership qualities necessary to manage a high-quality program successfully may prove very challenging. Having strong administrative support will be critical to this director's success.

> Staff development through training, communication, and leadership will be the crux for their producing an effective program.

At the top of any director's "To do" list is the hiring, training, supervising, and firing of staff. If the director has previously been a center teacher, this can be both a benefit and hindrance. It can be very helpful when you as a supervisor have walked in your staff's footsteps before. You can comprehend their positions and their challenges with greater understanding, and can offer support. This empathy can also backfire, though, and serve as a blinder toward seeing the whole picture and maintaining objectivity. Staff development through training, communication, and leadership will be the crux for their producing an effective program.

Did you know that for many centers, the director is also responsible for most, or all of the following?

- Planning and implementing curriculum

- Executing and possibly writing the center's budget

- Maintaining center enrollment

- Purchasing for the center

- Collecting and following up with tuition payments

- Developing policies and procedures

- Marketing and promotion of the center

- Upholding licensing standards and requirements

- Promoting strong community relations

- Managing the physical facility

- Having a working knowledge of legal standards for child care as they relate to the center

- Writing grants

- Managing parent communications and relations

- Coordinating the accreditation process

- Reporting to a board of directors

To be effective as an administrator, the director must be able to juggle these many responsibilities. Job burnout is high among these professionals. If supervisor support, advanced training, and peer networking are integrated into the position, it's more likely that the director will be successful. A good sign is a director who has been in the position for several years.

The Board of Directors

Many nonprofit child care centers include a board of directors. This board might be composed of community leaders and parents of the center. It behooves a program to solicit members with varied and specific expertise (lawyers, public relations professionals, accountants, construction, banking, physicians, etc.) to act as advisors and provide knowledge that will support the center. These leaders should also be representative of the cultural makeup of the community they serve.

The purpose of this board may be directly related to the child care center or to the larger organization to which the center belongs. The general functions of the board may include:

- Setting policy—determining how the program will function and establishing the process for that determination

- Planning for the short-term and long-term goals of the program

- Approving budget and capital expenditures

- Fund-raising

- Addressing pending problems

- Communicating with the administration, either directly or through the proper chain of command

Written policies and procedures (the bylaws) determine the structure of the board; how many members are required, their qualifications, and their responsibilities. Much of this is determined by the size of a center or organization. The bylaws will also specify the offices of the board (president, secretary, etc.) and their job descriptions.

A board of directors can contribute greatly to a program, but is usually connected with larger or more formally structured centers, and may not exist in smaller or privately owned ones. Smaller centers, though, have the opportunity to tap the existing parent body through other means and still benefit from their expertise.

Think about it. Could you be of assistance to your center either as a board member or in another active role?

Parent Advisory Committees

The strong partnership between a center and its families is the foundation of a council that can support the program and assist or advise the decision-making process. With the mutual agenda of the benefit and betterment of the program, Parent Advisory Committees (PACs) can represent the parents in the center concerning many issues. Each committee and center will determine its own function. Some ways that Parent Advisory Committees have provided this help:

- Communicating and interpreting policies

- Representing parent needs to the administration

- Providing staff recognition

- Acting as a class parent representative

- Initiating parent education programs

- Welcoming new families

- Holding social functions for the center

- Fund-raising

- Representing the center to the larger community

When a group like this works positively with a center, the results can only be a closer relationship between the two, and child care that is representative of its own families.

What you don't want to see is a parent body assembling out of anger to become a grievance committee. Efforts then are rarely effective, and can cause parents to separate from the administration rather than work together toward common goals. When specific issues of concern need to be addressed, it is better to have two representatives of the parent council sit down with the administration, express the agenda at hand, and look to brainstorm means of rectifying the problem, positively and jointly. This will dismantle the "us against them" attitude that can develop on both sides, and reduce the need for the administration to make a defensive response.

Child Care Workers

Who are they? They are changing dirty diapers, washing toys and tables, counting children, serving meals, and wiping dirty noses. They are helping soiled children who are without changes of clothing, writing in daily journals, and washing the spit-up off their clothes. They need to console sad children, redirect angry children, and are hit by other children. They must always think most carefully about their choice of words or actions before reacting to a situation. They receive poor pay, worse benefits, and little or no room for advancement. Is it any wonder that the child care field is high in turnover and low in attracting spirited and devoted new professionals?

Then, there is the smile and the dandelion that is just for them. The lonely tears that only they can make go away. That feeling of accomplishment they give by sensing when to step back, knowing it is independence they are fostering: for the playful nature they share; for the enticing experiences they provide; for the peace of mind they give to the parents; and for all the reasons that dedicated professionals stay in the field and strengthen its character.

> It is a very special person who will devote herself so lovingly to being a child care professional. This individual reaps her benefits from the warm relationships she is engaged in on a daily basis.

It is a very special person who will devote herself so lovingly to being a child care professional. This individual reaps her benefits from the warm relationships she is engaged in on a daily basis. Over my years in the profession, parents have shown their appreciation to their children's teachers and caregivers in numerous way. A small gift, a box of chocolates, a bagel breakfast. The most valued by the staff, though, have been the personal notes and letters parents took the time to write expressing sincere gratitude for the care they take of the children. It tells them, *somebody noticed.*

Often as parents we get caught up in trying to just get it all done, and don't stop to reflect on how we are doing it. Without good care for our children, we simply can't. When child care is successful, it is because of the caring individuals we entrust our children to every day. If you are fortunate enough to have found such care, find a way to make your appreciation known. That gesture signals your respect and recognition of their efforts and accomplishments.

The Center's Procedures

Rules and regulations and policies and forms and more forms and more rules! So many formalities seem to be required of you once you have entered the center's life. Do this, don't do that, and try to stay out of trouble with the director! What are the purposes behind these rules, and are they all really necessary?

Signing In and Out Every Day

Jessica's dad would walk in class, push his daughter toward the group of children, say, "See ya!" and then run out the door.

Monica's mom would pick her up at the end of the day while all the children were on the playground. Instead of returning to the class to pick up her child's things and sign her out, she would exit the playground in a hurry with her child in tow.

It was Chelsea's dad, though, whom I eventually caught in the act. Since he brought his daughter to the center during the peak drop-off time in the morning, many parents were in the room, and he often found it easy to slip out unnoticed.

Why was I in pursuit of each of these parents (along with many others)? After repeated requests, notes, and tailings, these parents were just refusing to sign their children in and out of the center each day. "I don't have time," or "Dropping off two children makes it difficult," or "The baby finally stopped crying. I just had to run!" While these are valid feelings and reasons for action, signing your children in and out of the center each day cannot and should not be overlooked.

The no-brainer to this dilemma is that most states require a center, by law, to have each child signed in and out each day. Where this is mandated, a center will be in noncompliance if they do not ensure your follow through, and the center will be cited as such. It is then the center's responsibility to journal each child's time of entry and departure, and who the accompanying adult was. Referencing this statute, however, did not change the practice of those parents at our centers who could not find the time or inclination to do it. The following excerpts from a letter I sent the parents did.

Just imagine the scenario. Your worst fears are realized. There is a fire. Fire alarms are sounding, and adults are rushing to get all children out of the building safely. This routine is practiced monthly, and the staff knows the details to it well. It's maybe

Child Care as an Extended Family

Though it's probably not found on your search and evaluation list, parents of young children usually find themselves in need of other families with similarly aged children. Maybe you have recently moved to the community and haven't had the opportunity to meet people, or perhaps you have been overloaded with a career up until this point, and hadn't stopped to notice the neighborhood around you! In this technological age, families are relocating around the country, often leaving family or friends behind. Merely knowing that you are not the only parent walking around with eyes glazed over from lack of sleep, or that there is a house to run to when you just feel like giving up, is a comfort that will sustain you through many challenges.

When child care works, families are comfortable with the adults taking care of their children. They feel they know them, trust them, occa-

nine o'clock in the morning, before the morning attendance has been logged. The only items staff will take outside with them, other than the children themselves, is the sign-in sheet and attendance book. Did you put your child right into her crib when you got to the center? Could your child be that one hiding under the table in the room? Though we would hope the adults in the room would be aware enough to know instinctively which children were currently there, perhaps in the midst of an emergency situation that might not be the case. I would always want to know that my child's name is on that sign-in sheet. When the count of children matches the names on the daily sign-in sheet, why would anyone look for another child left in the building?

The same scenario works in reverse, at the end of the day. Imagine having picked your child up at the end of the day, while she was on the playground. Just as the class is returning to the building, a fire erupts, and an evacuation follows. Upon

sionally look to them for advice, and know their own feelings and wishes are respected and followed. Families of the center begin to know each other from many different opportunities. It could be sitting on the train or bus together, walking through the parking lot of the center, meeting at birthday parties of children in your child's class or at social functions sponsored by the center. Getting to know these families provides a common bond. You are each entrusting your children daily with the same people at the same place, and are searching to balance the similar responsibilities of work, child care, and home. Your bond extends from the staff, to the center, to the children in the center, and to their families. Making sense of all the ins and outs of center life is certainly more encouraging when accompanied by the fellowship of others.

checking an attendance and sign-in sheet, there is no sign-out for your child. She is then assumed to be remaining in the building. Conflicting reports of your presence on the playground has staff questioning your having picked her up, and all efforts are made to return to the building to get her out.

It may be one extra step to take, and time is certainly a working parent's most valued commodity, but it is your responsibility to your child's safety to meticulously follow through with this detail consistently.

Any questions?

Discipline Policies

The manner in which children are dealt with and assisted in response to specific behaviors is discipline. It is your right as a parent to know how the center plans on dealing with your child in those instances. Each center should have a written statement declaring their policies for disciplining the children in the center. It should be available to parents, maybe hung in the lobby of the center, given to you upon registration, and included in each staff member's personnel file. This policy should not only tell you what the staff will do in those instances, but what they won't do as well. Look for a discipline policy that specifies that *the center will not:*

- Use corporal punishment of any kind under any circumstances
- Withhold food or bathroom privileges at any time
- Isolate a child without supervision
- Verbally abuse, threaten, humiliate, yell at, or intimidate a child

This policy should include how the center *will* respond to children:

- Make every effort to redirect or distract children, age appropriately
- Sit with children who need to be removed from a group
- Talk with children in a calm manner, attempting to understand the situation
- Use positive reinforcement
- Set reasonable expectations and offer logical consequences to behavior

Feel free to ask the director how the staff is trained in disciplining children. Staff at the center must have an understanding of each child's individual needs and his or her stage in development to respond appropriately. Discipline should be teaching opportunities, not punitive punishments. When a goal for children is *self-discipline,* the center is encouraging the child's responsibility for himself. That's an attribute we know many adults could benefit from!

Each center should have a written statement declaring their policies for disciplining the children in the center. It should be available to parents, maybe hung in the lobby of the center, given to you upon registration, and included in each staff member's personnel file.

Health Policies

There will be occasions when you will need to send in medicine to the center to be administered to your child in your absence. The center should have available a form for you to fill out, describing the reason for the medication, the name of it, and the proper dosage for the child. Please inform your center's staff each day that you send medication in. Even if you log it appropriately, and your child has been receiving it for several days previously, you want to ensure that staff are aware at all times. Never, ever, put the medicine in your child's lunch or daily tote for the teachers to discover. Children have been known to open childproof bottles, and accidents can occur. Each center or class should have one place that all medication will be stored.

Please understand the jeopardy staff put themselves in by taking the risk of making decisions without information from you, and try not to put them in such circumstances. Don't assume anything, and make sure you take the time to spell it all out and clarify your needs.

> Please inform your center's staff each day you are sending medication in.

Every center's health policy will have their own criteria for sending sick children home during the workday. I have seen a range in temperature elevation from barely 100 degrees to up to 102 degrees as the level at which a center will send a child home. Intestinal problems like diarrhea and vomiting are cause for sending children home. But is it after one episode that they must go home? Or the second, third, or fourth? Whatever your center's policy specifies, that's what you must abide by. If sick care is available at your center, you are not under as much stress as those working parents who have to shuffle and juggle on these occasions.

Childhood maladies like lice, hand, foot, and mouth disease, chicken pox, Giardia, strep throat, stomach viruses, and more can quickly go through a center. As a director, I shudder at the thought of each of them! You want to know in advance what symptoms to look for. Some ailments may require a doctor's note before your child can return to the center; others may just specify a period of time your child

As part of our nurturing of toddlers' self-help skills, the children are each encouraged to get their own lunch box, set it up in front of themselves, open it, and to eat their lunch. As Ms. Julia sat with the children, she was shocked to find Sarah's antibiotic medication in her open lunch box. She quickly removed the medicine, and ran to the medicine chart to check for its logging. When she realized it was not on the list, she called Sarah's parents at work. Neither of them was able to be reached. Messages were left for both. Without their authorization, Ms. Julia was unable to give the medication. When she received a call back several hours later, the parents said Sarah was supposed to have the medicine, but now it was too late, and she would have to miss a dose that day. They were most perturbed over our policy for administering medication, and blamed it for Sarah's relapse of her ear infection a week later.

must remain out of the center. Find out if notices are sent home when there have been children in the center with contagious diseases. This is not an unusual request at all, and most centers probably do this as part of their regular practice.

Late Fees

Probably the most complaints I've heard over the years are about extra fees that are assessed when parents pick their children up late. A center will have fixed hours that parents are well aware of and the staff expects to work within.

Though most parents are very respectful and appreciative, there are those few parents who will take advantage of the center and staff's presence by continually picking their children up late. Late fees do not scare them. This clearly signals a lack of respect for those people caring for their children.

na's dad arrived just over an hour late one evening. He had been held up in traffic and did not stop to call. When the overtime bill came to his home, he was outraged, and called me. He argued that it was not his fault that there was an accident during his commute home and therefore should not be penalized with an absurd late fee. I did recognize his situation, and acknowledged that we were aware he did not choose to be late. However, the adults taking care of his child did not choose to stay late either. They needed to be financially compensated for staying with his child past closing hours. Staff were calling all around trying to locate him or one of the adults listed as an alternate pick-up in his daughter's file. Their evening plans were disrupted, but they were professional and made Ana's time go quickly for her.

I did not remind him that the center is under obligation to call the police if a child is not picked up, or if the center has been unable to make contact with an authorized pick-up person an hour after the center closes. He just missed that deadline. Yes, this was an unplanned evening; unfortunately the unexpected can always come up, and odds are in larger centers they usually will. If one parent doesn't have to pay a late fee when he is stuck in traffic, why should the next parent pay it?

Center staff work very long hours and are usually tired at the end of their day. They have their own families, and they look forward to going home to them and ending their day at the center. Respect their personal lives, and do not take advantage of their presence at the center.

Internet Monitoring Services

There are many new innovative services and products available for child care centers. Among those receiving much attention is an Internet

Leo's dad was always late picking him up, anywhere from ten to thirty minutes. Of course, Leo was aware he was the only child in the center for that period of time. The staff came to me complaining about his lateness. Even though he was being charged a dollar a minute, Leo's dad appeared to make little or no effort to arrive on time. It took me several conversations with him, and promise of his son's removal from our program, before he was able to pick his son up within our operating hours.

monitoring service. It works like this: Installed in each of the classrooms are video cameras that the center purchases or leases from a security company. These cameras take pictures of the classroom approximately every ten seconds. These pictures are then sent to an Internet service that is accessed with a password by those subscribing to the service. There is no sound accompanying the pictures. The centers pay for the set up of the service and the equipment, and parents purchase subscriptions to log on to the Web site.

While at the computer at their office or home, Mom and Dad can log on and check in on their child. Centers using this have reported great success from parents and center's point of view. After initially hearing about this new service, I enthusiastically brought it to our parents, expecting their eager response as well. However the more we learned about it, the more uncertainty parents, staff, and I all had about it.

The *pluses* of an Internet monitoring service, as our center saw them:

- For the parents: Peace of mind at being able to observe their child in the center any time, especially if traveling, if transition that morning was difficult, or if other concerns are peaked. New parents missing their baby are provided with an additional link, so they can feel more a part of their child's day.

- For the center: Parent trust is maximized as they are able to share the day and see for themselves the wonderful things going on. Pride in the center is at its pinnacle.

We then found the *minuses* of an Internet monitoring service:

- For the parents: First, the biggest objection was that if they did not want their child photographed, the child could not be excluded from this video link. Second, many parents do not have access to the Internet during their workday. Among those that did, several felt they would be addicted to the screen (not doing their work), and always questioning what they saw, since there is no audio. Third, although I am told there is no risk of this, parents were concerned about pedophiles gaining access and watching their children on the Internet. And last, as one parent expressed to me, "If I can't trust where my child is and who they are with to the point I feel the need to check up on him or the center, then he is in the wrong place."

- For the center: Too many opportunities for misinterpretation of circumstances, since audio is not always included and pictures can be fragmented. The need to explain situations continually is potentially high. Costs associated with installation are high.

Parents were clearly divided on their opinions of this service, with three-quarters of our families seeing more negatives than positives. Technology is changing and making advancements. New services yet to be tested widely in the market are making their way onto the horizon. They include full audio and visual monitoring of classrooms. If your center has a service like this, or is investigating its inclusion, find out as much as you can about it so your voice will be an educated one.

Licensing

The state may have given the center a license, but that should not be interpreted as an endorsement of any kind. Each state has its own criteria for child care centers and will have its own methods for overseeing and ensuring that those laws are being followed. I would not even consider a center-based program that does not have a valid state license, but don't let possession of that license override your own investigation into a center either.

The common focus for licensing is divided between two key areas: 1) facility, health, and safety; and 2) programming.

What is considered safe depends upon where you are in the country. Traditionally, facilities caring for children under two-and-a-half years old must comply with additional building requirements than those providing for older children. This is to ensure that the younger, more-dependent children are safe during emergencies. Number of exits, bathrooms, and the condition of walls, floors, plumbing, and lighting all fall under the physical requirement codes for a town and state. Those state inspectors from programming or life and safety divisions will rarely make an appearance to a center unless their licensing is up for renewal, or a complaint has been logged. Local health and building officials will make routine inspections under similar circumstances.

Programming conditions will cover areas like ratios and group size, staff requirements, and curriculum.

A center may be in non-compliance for several things on an inspection. Health records may find several children needing updated immunizations, a tear in the carpeting might be cited for repair, a garbage can in the bathroom may have a missing lid, and a soap dispenser might need refilling. All these things will be cited as infractions of the requirements, but are not considered threatening to a center's license at all. If the soap dispenser is refilled while the inspector is at the site, that citation will note its abatement at the time of visit. Reinspection at a later date will validate if other items have been taken care of within the specified period of time. Centers will be issued temporary licenses until all violations are abated. Once a center is in full compliance, a perma-

It was one of those days at the center. The teacher of our three-year-olds became violently ill during the class, and literally had to bolt from the school. As she ran out the door, she brushed passed the state inspector who was just entering our building. Naturally, the inspector instinctively was drawn to that class of three-year-olds first. Upon entering the room, she counted seventeen three-year-olds with just one teacher. State ratio for three-year-olds in New Jersey is one to ten. We were in the middle of trying to move staff and cover the absent teacher's position, but the inspector still cited us for being out of ratio. She then abated the citation five minutes later when we were able to find coverage for the room.

Although there was abatement at the time of visitation, that violation still appeared on our record. It surfaced as abated without cause for further investigation, but still raised questions for the few parents doing their own investigations.

nent license is issued. This license will be valid for a set amount of time, based on that state's law.

There are those centers, however, whose infractions of licensing are far more serious than a soap dispenser in need of soap. These centers may have physical obstacles within their building that need to be rectified, or programming problems such as too many children in a room. Though licensing will seek to assist a program in overcoming these challenges, they will not be forgiving of a center that jeopardizes the safety, health, or well-being of any child.

When doing your search and evaluation, check with the Bureau of Licensing in your state and request a list of outstanding violations (if any) that center has. Don't necessarily prejudge a center based on those citations; ask licensing and the center's director to provide more information to you that is specific to those infractions.

Though some infractions do not have to mean a center is of poor quality, they should never be ignored. Your own observations and feelings, weighed with those additional pieces of information from licensing, will assist your ability to make an educated and informed decision.

Fund-raising

I rarely come across a parent who relishes the thought of soliciting other people for their child's center. When parents hear that term, *fund-raising,* they usually try and duck for fear of being volunteered for something! The unfavorable news is, most centers will do some form of fund-raising at least once, usually twice during a year. Many of you will react with distaste at this thought, and feel your tuition dollars should not require you to go out and hawk goods for your child's center. "With the tuition you charge, and those waiting lists, you should have plenty to buy whatever the center needs!" one friendly new parent notified me as our fall fund-raiser was underway.

There are many different types of fund-raising a center will do, depending on its size, needs, and function. You may find your center fund-raising for:

- New playground equipment
- Fresh books and toys for the center
- Staff training
- A new building
- Furnishings for existing or additional classrooms
- Field trips
- Enrichment opportunities for the center
- Scholarship assistance for less-fortunate families

You could find yourself peddling anything from candy bars and cheesecakes to flower bulbs, raffles, or wrapping paper.

Some centers will take the straight approach and just asked for donations through phone-a-thons or face-to-face solicitations. There are also those parents who prefer not to participate in a *sale,* but will make a personal donation instead. Many programs have orchestrated special events like auctions, flea markets, and concerts. These not only raise money for the center, but they also add to the community effort and gathering of the center's families.

In some centers I know, a bare playground would never have had the opportunity to be built up and enhanced without fund-raising dollars. Other inner-city preschoolers would not have been able to take class trips to see special shows. Teachers would not have benefited from additional staff training. There has been replacement of old or broken appliances, carpeting, library books, and infant toys. These purchases would have not been possible had parents not unified for the centers' fund-raisers.

Parents, teachers, and administration should all have a voice in the decision-making process when it comes time to spend the money.

Tuition

Where *does* your tuition go? Why is all this fund-raising needed? Shouldn't all the money you are paying cover all those things needed for the center?

In traditionally run businesses, we expect a budget to cover daily operational expenses as well as anything else that business might need to succeed. When budgets do not allow for the additional succeeding line items, that business does without. We certainly don't expect to walk into a supermarket and see an employee or a customer selling candy bars so they can remodel the store! In the case of child care businesses, though, the budget is typically very lopsided, with rare opportunities to include enhancements. Then it is our children who are doing without.

Salary-related costs are the highest portion of a child care budget, and will run anywhere from 70 to 90 percent. There is not much room left for updating old and broken furniture and equipment, buying new toys and books, and training staff.

As much as you are paying for your child care (and wherever you live, it is expensive), believe it or not, you are probably not paying enough. Although expensive child care is not always good quality child care, for child care to be good quality, it will be expensive! The lower the child to teacher ratios, the more qualified the staff, and the better the facility, the more it will cost to operate. When between 70 and 90 percent of an operating budget is allocated to staff salaries and benefits, you would hope that those workers are being compensated well. The saddest part about that, though, is that child care workers continue to be the lowest-paid category of workers in this country, despite the fact that they have a higher level of education than the average worker does!

> Salary-related costs are the highest portion of a child care budget, and will run anywhere from 70 to 90 percent.

Many child care workers have college and post-graduate degrees!

Even with those sorry statistics, most child care center budgets are eaten up with salary-related costs. What's left? Take the balance for operational costs like building rent, heat, and phone, then include marketing and promotion, consumable supplies like paper, crayons, and glue, food when applicable, maintenance, and throw in the increasingly high costs of insurance for child care centers. Most centers operate on a very thin margin. Without sharp financial management skills, many find it difficult to maintain their existence. A center that has been operating successfully for five years or more at least has a proven track record, and is likely to be around for the next five or more years.

There are centers receiving funding from the United Way and other charitable agencies, and government-funded Head Start programs are able to offer a reduced tuition or sliding fee scale based on income level. Though their budgets include income from sources other than the families they serve, the breakdown of expenses will still be disproportionately high on costs associated with payroll.

Reality Check

Try not to blow your top about the child care center's administration or practices. There are times when the energy is worth it, and times when

The preschool teacher had warned me, but I just couldn't relate to this parent's fury. Many letters had been sent home requesting that the parents send children to the center in easy casual clothing that was OK to get dirty. We play in the dirt on the playground, with paints and clay, and we don't want children to feel inhibited by their clothing or to ruin and soil their good clothes! Kristen's mom had expressed concern over her getting messy. After several pleas for play clothes and sneakers from the teacher were denied, the staff tried to accommodate this mom by following Kristen around attempting to protect her from any mess! Her mother came in to the center late one afternoon. This was probably the angriest I can remember ever seeing a parent.

"Look! Just look at her shoes! I just bought these Mary Janes a week ago, and look!" She was shaking the shoes in my face as she was hollering at me, with Kristen by her side. The black patent leather shoes had mud on them, their reflection all but gone. "How can you let her go into a mud puddle? I was very specific that I did not want her near any mud! Now look at them! What am I going to do with these? Huh? What do you think I should do with these shoes now?"

A little shocked by her reaction, I couldn't help but reply, "I guess you could try cleaning them," when suddenly she looked like she was going to burst a blood vessel. She then grabbed Kristen's arm (who looked positively mortified) and stormed out of my office.

it is not. Too often, if a parent loses sight of what is important to them, their response to a situation appears inappropriate. Other times it is a very appropriate response. Maybe it was a tough day at work, or perhaps you did not sleep the night before. It could be just the need to pull in the reigns as you feel you are losing control. We all have visions of what we want for our children, and settling for someone else's vision for our child is not something we expect to have to do.

Keep the communication flowing and frequent. It will help minimize misunderstandings and ensure your needs are being met. The director of your center cannot be everywhere at all times. She relies on constructive feedback from parents to do her job! Your sharing information with her, complaints as well as compliments, is very valuable to an administrator who is always seeking to improve the program. Bringing uncomfortable situations to the attention of the director *before* they become problems can often avoid much difficulty.

Within each program, you should be made aware of philosophy, policies, and practice. When there is a questionable match, you have the option of finding a different center that shares your beliefs, or rethinking and modifying yours to meet the expectations of the center. However, if you are aware of a center's practice and philosophy, but choose not to subscribe to it, be prepared for some challenging occasions.

> Bringing uncomfortable situations to the attention of the director *before* they become problems can often avoid much difficulty.

It is certainly understandable for a parent to want to pick their child up nice and clean at the end of the day. Clothes are expensive and not easily replaced as well. *But the reality is: Kids will get dirty!* As much as we may try and monitor those puddles on the playground, you can be sure that a few children will find them. Sand is bound to come home in shoes and hair when your pick-up hour is your child's time outside. Even with smocks that cover as much as they can, be prepared for paints to find their way to the child's shirt. Unless you plan on putting a body bib on your four-year-old, you can be guaranteed that juice will land on his lap at some point. Don't set your children up for failure and anxiety over getting themselves dirty, and don't set yourself up for disappointment by sending in your newborn wearing ruffles and bows! Keep clothing simple and inexpensive. If you need to pick your child up in good clothes, see that they have plenty of changes of more comfortable clothing and shoes so they can relax and enjoy their day, then ask staff to have them changed and ready upon your arrival.

The fact is, everyone has their own distinctive style. Each family has the right to want things a particular way. Sometimes it can be difficult, though, for child care providers to relate to the requests and needs of certain parents, if the workers do not subscribe to similar thought. Be clear in making your needs known, and ascertain whether the response from your provider is one which you support. If it is not, then you need to either rethink your request or your child care. It is less likely that your provider will rethink the philosophy of the program.

Following a few simple rules of thumb might aid your ability to determine if a situation warrants blowing your top. Choose your battles carefully and ask yourself:

- Am I pleased with the overall care my child is receiving?

- Is my child in safe, healthy, nurturing, and capable arms every day?

- Is the program respectful and considerate of the individual families?

- Is my child happy?

If you can answer "Yes" to all of these, then ask yourself:

- Does this situation affect or compromise any of the above?

- If I overlook this issue, will the problem further escalate or trigger others?

A negative response to these might indicate your need to reevaluate the circumstances and find a more effective method to convey your feelings. Affirmation of these predicaments confirms your need to approach the center and attempt to clarify and rectify the situation. If you answered the first set of questions negatively, you need to reexamine your child care situation more broadly than the idiosyncrasies you currently find yourself bothered with.

6

The Survival

Babies and Toddlers

I have been told many times by parents of this age group that raising a child would be so much easier if only their child would communicate in words! We measure our young babies and toddlers' successes the only way we know how, as an interpretation viewed from our adult world. We need to be reminded that babies, just as adults, all have different needs and desires. By imposing our own needs and desires on our babies, we may be asking them to conform to a standard or practice that is not conducive to their personality style. I believe each child comes to us with his own set of rules, only we don't get a copy of that rule book! It is up to us, as parents and caregivers, to be sensitive to our babies and to figure out what our children need from us and from the outside world. We can then respond in a manner that is supportive of them.

As you and your child stroll through each stage, try not to lose sight of whose issues you are challenging. Ask frequently, "Is this a benefit to my child? Or perhaps it is a perceived benefit, but really derived from my own needs as a parent?" Keep in mind that some of the things we want to do as parents fulfill our own needs. "Do I want this to help me transition, to separate more easily, to feel closer or more involved to my child's day?" And then ask yourself, "Does it have an unraveling effect on my baby?" Though both parent's and child's needs count, when we ask ourselves these questions, we are then better prepared to act more objectively, satisfying both the parent and the child.

The Program

What is developmentally appropriate practice for infants and toddlers? When knowledge of child development is integrated into child care practice, a greater understanding of age appropriateness and readiness is a natural result. In chapter 2, "The Search," we explained the term *developmentally appropriate practice* (DAP) as it refers to children generally. Within each age group, DAP will have different characteristics. But the one common denominator will continue to be a child-initiated, caregiver-supported approach to play and caregiving.

Care for the youngest babies revolves around their security. This is formed when there is close contact with loving and responsive caregivers. Out with that theory our grandparents had, that if we hold our babies too long or pick them up too soon we are spoiling them. On the contrary, we are giving them reason to trust that someone will respond to their needs. We are giving them the warmth and assurance they need to feel contented and thrive.

> Out with that theory our grandparents had, that if we hold our babies too long or pick them up too soon we are spoiling them.

As younger babies grow into older babies, the security they have gained allows them to venture out a bit from their caregivers and explore the safe environment around them. Those caregivers, however, should only be a glance away when baby checks over her shoulder for that reassurance of availability to her. As this baby develops her identity, venturing further and further out, choices are provided and limits are set. Independence in the making!

The Environment

Both young babies and toddlers depend on the environment to function as their curriculum. Keep in mind, however, that as long as safety is a priority and never compromised, wonderful care may still be given in less than optimum surroundings. Though the setting is an important component, it is the people taking care of these young children who will have the greatest effect on the quality of care received, not the presence of a water table, a new changing table, or a fancy climber.

Entering these rooms, warm, neutral colors on the walls and floors might be accented by brighter colors of soft cushions and the children's family pictures hung at their eye level. Looking at others in childproof mirrors engages almost any baby in delight! A short tunnel offers opportunity for a little peek-a-boo with a caregiver. Risers or low climbing structures initiate crawling and exploration. Carpeted floor space for creeping and playing is available, and gross motor skills get their work out! Toys are age-appropriate and available for mobile babies and toddlers. Several of the same kinds of toys are available to children so as to avoid tug-of-war episodes and shelves are not stuffed with items.

Swings, walkers, playpens, and other contraptions do not take up any room here since it's the caregivers who provide the attention and responsiveness that these babies crave. The rocking chair in the room quietly awaits a hungry or sleepy baby to be nurtured by his caregiver. It is this kind of space and furnishings that entice young crawlers and new walkers into safe opportunities for exercising their growing muscles.

Working with Child Care Staff

Though parents become reliant on information from the center on a daily basis, they often fail to realize how the staff also depends on information from them.

For instance, when one of the infant caregivers showed me a rash on a five-month-old baby, we called the parents to let them know what we had discovered. They proceeded to inform us that baby had received her immunizations immediately prior to arriving at the center that day. Another time one of our toddlers was having a very aggressive week, looking to hurt his friends at every opportunity. We confronted Mom with this change in behavior, asking for her assistance, only to find out that there had been a very violent scene at home between this toddler's parents. The evening before the aggression had begun, Dad had been taken away by the police, and this toddler had been witness to it.

Had the center been informed that baby had received his shots, the staff would have been checking carefully for reactions on a more regular basis. We were fortunate that the staff noticed the rash when they did. If staff had known about even a little of the violence the toddler witnessed, they might have been able to anticipate some of his fury, and perhaps help him work through it with a greater understanding and sensitivity. It is not necessary to share intimate details of personal family life. That is certainly one's own business. Knowing that the child had a bad experience, however, or that he is under an unusual amount of stress will aid staff in offering appropriate support.

Our center came up with some strategies that helped overcome a bit of this for the babies. We asked parents to fill out a quick checklist on a daily basis. This list asked simple questions about baby's sleep the night before, times of waking and bedtime, any changes in schedule, medication being given at home, and any general concerns parents may have. Though this certainly does not provide for full disclosure of information, it aided staff in knowing baby better, and thereby they offered more sympathetic and responsive care. Try suggesting a similar checklist to your center.

> Though the setting is an important component, it is the people taking care of these young children who will have the greatest affect on the quality of care received, not the presence of a water table, a new changing table, or a fancy climber.

Making the time to communicate and share pertinent issues with your child's caregivers can be difficult. If you are both rushed during the morning drop-off, ask when would be a good time for you to call. Or write a note to the caregivers conveying your message: "Sammy seemed under-the-weather this morning though he has no fever—please call if he continues to appear irritable." This little extra effort will not only be appreciated by the staff, but will serve in your child's best interests, and add to your very much-needed peace of mind.

Special Needs

Some children come to the center with special circumstances. Most facilities should be able to accommodate those circumstances, and be willing to assist families as long as a physician has determined it is safe for this special needs child to be in group care.

At our centers, we have successfully integrated premature babies, babies on heart monitors and apnea medication, babies with casts and braces on their legs. We have taken care of babies on radioactive medication that required staff to take additional precautionary measures when diapering, toddlers on breathing nebulizers for asthma, children with hearing aids, ADHD children, and more.

When you have been given the medical go-ahead, make your needs known to the director and staff. The more people at the center who are informed and educated about your child's special needs, the better taken care of he will be. Spend time at the center showing them how to work an apparatus, give a medication, or reason with your emotional child. How you get the attention of your hearing-impaired child will be of great value to the staff. Sharing the parts of your child's leg brace with the class is a great way to make the other children comfortable with it.

Babies in Child Care

The Staff

When we walk into the baby rooms, we see caregivers respectful of when baby needs "count the toes" time, discovering himself through uninterrupted peaceful moments. We notice staff to be intuitively responsive when he is playfully energized and waiting for interaction. Ba-

> ## Red Light Warning
>
> When a caregiver's response to a crying baby is to shake a rattle in the baby's face and say, "You're OK—OK—you're OK," as they stare off into the room.

bies are active participants in the group setting. There are opportunities for her to solve her own problems. A *crawler,* with eyes intent on reaching a toy, is allowed to pursue his quest without adult interference. Routine rituals are not routine, as baby and caregiver engage in conversation and games during diaper changes and meals. Babies are told what is going to happen before it does, giving them time to anticipate and adjust. Staff never leave a baby to cry in a crib nor to sit for extended periods in infant seats. These babies learn to trust and feel safe because caregivers respond to them in a loving and timely manner. They are held and carried; caregivers are sensitive to what baby needs. Bottles are given to young babies in adult arms, and are never propped. Voices are generally soft and pleasing.

Nursing Your Child Care Baby

Yes, you *can* still nurse after you return to the workforce, but preparations need to be made for you and baby to be successful. It is critical that your baby is comfortable taking a bottle by the time you return to work. A nursing baby who doesn't know what to do with a bottle is a hungry baby in someone else's arms. Very often, parents will introduce a bottle just a week or two before their baby enters the child care program. They panic as the assortment of nipples and bottles pile up, none of them seeming to be the *right* one! While some babies might instinctively do well on a bottle, many need additional time and nurturing through this transition. After all, Mom is much softer, warmer, and loving! Why should baby take an impersonal piece of latex or silicone if

Mom is close by? Give your baby and yourself at least a month of tak-ing a supplemental bottle. Have another family member introduce it several times each day, otherwise your scent will be picked up and con-fuse the baby. If you are out of the room initially, it makes it less dis-tracting, and baby will be less likely to resist it.

Is your baby going to be on breast milk while you are at work, or for-mula? If it will be formula, you need to be sure that the formula is the right one for your baby. Again, I suggest at least a month of supplemen-tal formula bottles prior to the start of child care. Rid yourself (and the center) of any doubts of allergies or gastric problems before the big day.

When bottles for the center are going to be filled with breast milk, get yourself comfortable using a good pump. Though there are em-ployers that provide opportunity for nursing employees to use a breast pump, such employers are, not surprisingly, in the minority. Of course, many women may find it awkward and uncomfortable to pump during the workday. For those mothers whose employers have provided con-venience and support for you to manage this easily, I highly encourage it. Though it is time-consuming, pumping while away from baby will mean he will get the maximum amount of breast milk from you he can. Many of the moms at our center have also found success by doing

all their daily pumping before and after work. These women found they were still able to maintain a good milk supply. They pumped enough for a day's worth of bottles, plus additional amounts on the weekends to add to a freezer back-up supply. (A must have!) Remember, at 0 degrees Fahrenheit, breast milk can be stored for several months! If you are one of the lucky ones who work around the corner or in the same building as your child's center, you have the luxury of nursing your baby in the middle of the day.

Visiting Your Baby

Parents will frequently ask me if it is OK to visit their baby during the day, or if Grandma lives close by, could she occasionally drop in to say hello? Parents and grandparents should always be welcome visitors to a center. At no time should a center tell you that you cannot visit your child. Any center that restricts visitations from parents should be crossed off your scouting list. Immediately!

> Any center that restricts visitations from parents should be crossed off your scouting list. Immediately!

There is a caveat to this, however. Your child may not be overcome with joy at your sudden appearance during *his* day, especially if it is not part of his routine. Or he may not fare well after you depart. There are many factors that will influence your child's ability to integrate your visitation into his day successfully. Some you will have control of, others you will not.

With the best of intentions, parents and grandparents will stop by the center in the middle of the day if their work schedule permits. It is a very secure feeling to be able to pop in unannounced and check up on baby. While some children will handle this interruption easily, most will have a difficult time after their visitor leaves. Babies and young children need to anticipate their world. When visitors have been in, baby may look toward the entrance for the rest of the day, expecting another surprise visit from Mom. Be sure to communicate with your child's caregivers about his reaction after such a visit. You will then possess the knowledge you need to decide how you would like to handle future visits.

As it happened, two mothers of infants in the same nursery worked locally and were able to visit with their babies during their lunch breaks. The babies had each started in the nursery at just a few months old. For one baby, James, this routine became very natural for him. James would start looking around in anticipation every day at eleven thirty when Mom would arrive. When she did arrive, it was a joyous time for both! Mom would give James his bottle, play with him, and sometimes settle him down for his nap. The days she left before he went to sleep, he fussed for just a moment and then was easily distracted by his caregiver as he resumed his normal routine. As he got older, he looked forward to Mom's arrival, shared lunch and his friends with her, and then was lulled into slumber as Mom rubbed his back to the classical music playing in the background. When James awoke, he was well-rested and happy. Mom had routinely not been present when he awoke from his nap, so he did not anticipate her presence at this time. On the rare occasion when Mom had a meeting and could not keep their routine, the staff would tell James that Mom couldn't be there that day for lunch, but would see him at the end of the day as always. For reasons I'll never really know, James was never thrown off. It didn't appear to make him cranky or keep him from eating and resting as he typically would. He joyfully accepted his mother when she was there, parted with her when the time came, and managed well if a break in their routine came up.

> The most successful of child care experiences are the result of communication between home and center.

The other baby, Brandon, had a very different experience integrating his mom with child care. As a most playful baby, when Brandon's mom would arrive for lunch, he naturally was very happy to see her. Mom nursed him, played with him, took him for a walk, then returned him to the arms of his primary caregiver and went back to work. Brandon's behavior and mood took on the characteristics of a different child in the afternoons. It took a long time for the caregiver to settle Brandon down for a nap. He would fuss, cry, and had a most difficult time being consoled. We spoke with Brandon's mom about the change in his behavior after she would leave the center. We asked for some suggestions that might assist us in helping Brandon during this difficult transition. She was most cooperative in trying to brainstorm with us ways to make the afternoons easier for Brandon. Even when he would awake after his nap, his mood was fussy all afternoon. A day came when Brandon's mom had to miss a visit. We were startled to find that not only did his lunch without Mom go fine, but his afternoon was much better than it had been! Just the change in his schedule should have been enough to throw him off. When Mom did arrive at the end of the day, we tactfully shared Brandon's successful afternoon and suggested that maybe breaking the daily routine, when Mom would take him for a walk and leave the center, was more than Brandon was able to handle at this time. Did she want to consider changing the routine to see how he did? Perhaps not leave the building with him during her visits? (We believed that was at the crux of Brandon's difficulties.) She responded that she cherished these walks with Brandon every afternoon and did not want to spend her time with him at the center. "He'll get over it," she said. We supported her decision and tried to make Brandon's afternoons as happy and loving as we could.

When you come to the decision whether, how, and when to visit your baby, consider his temperament, feedback from his caregivers, and your personal requirements. We know children don't come to the center alone, they come to us with their families. We hope that your center will put the family high on the priority list. As a parent, you count too! Upsetting your child for an afternoon may not be the greater value here. So when you weigh each of these factors, consider your needs as a valid and important influence too.

Your Primary Caregiver

She affectionately takes your baby out of your arms when you signal that you're ready to leave. She senses when his mood is out of character, that possibly he's getting sick or teething, and calls you at work to discuss. She faithfully writes in baby's daily log, and shares this information with you. She has built a bond of trust with you and your baby. She is your baby's primary caregiver.

A primary caregiver should be assigned to babies newborn up to at least two years old. This caregiver is the one person whom baby truly gets an opportunity to become attached to and trust. Though this is the adult mostly responsible for taking care of your baby and communicating with you, it does not mean that your child will not get to know other staff members. If your baby wakes up from his nap, and his primary caregiver is tending to another baby, he should not be left to cry and wait until his primary caregiver is available. Rather, another staff member should get him up and confer with baby's caregiver about his needs at that time. This staff member should be able to help out until his primary caregiver is again available. He gets to know and feel comfortable with other staff members, but most likely has a special bond with just one.

Why is this primary care system so important? As discussed in chapter 9, "The Success," babies need to form secure attachments with their caregivers in order to feel safe and be able to forecast their environment. Babies who sense the rhythms of their caregivers and the routines of their day are less likely to worry with anticipation. By developing a special relationship together, baby and caregiver not only delight in each other's company, but depend on it for baby's success.

Parents, too, benefit greatly when primary caregivers are in place. A relationship develops that allows for the easy exchange of information. There isn't the constant need to explain your baby's temperament and habits to someone. The primary caregiver knows and understands your baby. Look for each caregiver to be assigned to babies who are on different schedules or babies of a wider range in age. This provides for her not having to diaper, feed, and soothe three or four babies at the same time. Ask how caregivers are paired with families. Before you are assigned to a specific caregiver, request a match with one whose work schedule overlaps with yours. This could be the beginning of the day or the end, and will ensure maximum opportunity for exchanging information face to face.

Communication and Information Sharing

In the best of care situations, if the communication between center and home is not accurate and dependable, it will be cause for uneasiness. If the center's staff does not share information about your child's day freely, how will you be able to incorporate his experiences of her time away from you into your life at home? The most successful of child care experiences are the result of communication between home and center: parents sharing the sleepless night they had because baby was teething and cranky; staff communicating that baby pulled on his ear all afternoon. The information exchanged provides both parents and caregivers the necessary tools they need to ensure baby's happiness and health.

What Do I Need to Know on a Daily Basis?

Every center has its own system for reporting daily information. Our center has each parent provide a marble *notebook* that staff uses for daily entries for infants and young toddlers. These notebooks become wonderful keepsakes of baby's infancy and toddler years. Many centers use *daily sheets* as their reporting system. As long as you are getting the information you need, both systems work fine. There are the obvious bits of knowledge you want to ensure you are receiving.

- **Food and bottle intake** are important for parents of babies to know. Expect that each feeding should be listed with the time and amount of food or formula taken. Staff should also make note if baby spits up a lot after meals. If there are extreme discrepancies between eating patterns at home and at the center, you may want to discuss this with the caregiver. Though usually well-intentioned, a staff member may give the baby more or less food than you think is necessary. You would notice this immediately upon reading baby's daily sheet. To avoid any problems, discuss immediately with the staff member and make sure your wishes are being followed.

- **Frequency of diaper changes** should also be marked by time, and include notes about any unusual bowel movements (diarrhea, hard stools, etc.). If your toddler is concentrating on potty readiness, this progress should also be reported.

- **Nap times and length** should be noted. If baby is mixing up his days and nights, this information becomes valuable as parent and staff brainstorm to ease a change in baby's sleep patterns. Even the amount of time napping for toddlers should be reported with accuracy.

- **What baby did today** is fun to hear about. It's always nice to know the names of the songs the staff are singing with the babies, the titles of the stories they enjoy together, and the type of art projects they do together. There is a recognition when you sing that song or read that story with baby at home. Knowing some of his experiences offers an opening for dialog with your toddler: "How did the sand feel mixed in with the finger paints?" The most valuable information though, is when staff are able to articulate your child's personal interactions: how he clapped his hands with joy during the song; how she wanted to turn the pages and take the book away from the caregiver; and how your toddler started sponge painting his arms in fascination instead of the paper on the table! If the center is not communicating this well, try to discuss what you want to hear about with them. Not all personnel will able to express this adequately in written form. Have patience; it may take a few tries, but eventually they will be better able to meet your needs.

The information received daily is priceless for most parents. They can't wait to see what has been written in their child's notebook at the conclusion of the day! Not all staff will have the communication skills to meet your needs, though. That doesn't mean this is representative of the care your child received that day. Taking the time to get to know the staff will help you determine what you expect and require from them.

Illnesses

The biggest challenge in any group care environment is limiting the exchange of germs to children. When babies are still immobile, that exchange is minimal and so *should* be the number of illnesses. Unfortunately, as the child begins to crawl, walk, and move around, he is touching surfaces, flooring, toys, and other babies. When the center is diligent about washing and sanitizing toys after they have been in baby's mouth, hand washing for the staff and the children; wearing gloves during soiled diaper changes, nose wiping, and food serving; and sanitizing surfaces, you're off to a good start. But as babies touch each

I've heard Evelyn writes the best books! Is it possible to get Evelyn as Rosie's primary caregiver? I don't want Caroline though; I hear she's nice, but her spelling and grammar are atrocious, and she writes the same things in the books all the time." Evelyn was a wonderful caregiver for Rosie, only her hours were such that she never saw Rosie's mom or dad. As it turned out, Rosie sought comfort in Caroline's arms each morning when her mom left. Mom and Caroline developed a warm rapport and exchanged anecdotes and stories daily. Rosie's mom came to me several months later. "I never should have sold Caroline short based on hearsay and her ability to write in the books. Evelyn is wonderful and all, but Caroline does so much more for Rosie and me each day. I know now there is more to being a good caregiver than the ability to articulate in these notebooks.

other while their hands are in their mouths and who knows where else, germs will rapidly spread.

Every child is so different, and it is almost impossible to predict which children will be the ones to be chronically ill during that first year of group care. Also as difficult to predict are the children who will get by with just one or two colds that year. I think it is safe to assume that if your child has not had any exposure to the public, germs, and illness, beginning group care will trigger an onset of some illness. One of the biggest challenges I face as an administrator is keeping sick children out of the center. Though all of the sanitation procedures take much effort for staff, there are also concrete things that can be done to minimize health problems. There is then the follow-up to ensure that they are being practiced. These practices are within the controls of a center. When a child wakes up from his nap with a fever, and has already spread his germs around, the situation falls out of the control boundaries.

One little boy in our center had a chronic runny nose, the *colorful* kind. Though he never ran a fever, rarely did he appear well. Every morning Gregory's parent's brought him in, the parents of other children around him would shudder. His eyes would be puffy, his nose would be packed with mucus, his breathing was labored, and he appeared tired. When staff approached his parents, questioning Gregory's health, they said he had allergies, had been up late the night before, or had a little cold, but was fine. I found myself sending him home once a week, requesting a doctor's note saying he was not contagious and was well enough to be in child care. To my surprise, they always came through with a doctor's note saying just that. He never returned with any medication. With the parents' permission, I even called the doctor's office to request more detailed information about Gregory's allergies. I also wanted to make sure the physician had seen him, and the note was not just a result of a nurse accommodating a parent. Yes, Gregory had been seen! Well, I was absolutely shocked. This child was ill. I was worried for the health of other children he might contaminate as well as our own ability to care for him while his breathing was so labored. Not being a physician, I had to rely on the words of the pediatrician sending him back to care, and the words of my own sick-child policy coming back to haunt me. (After that incident, I did add "at the discretion of the director" under reasons for sending an ill child home to our sick-child policy.)

> The information received daily is priceless for most parents. They can't wait to see what has been written in their child's notebook at the conclusion of the day!

Happily for Gregory, his parents did change doctors shortly thereafter, and with antibiotics, he was finally well. I often wondered why, though, these parents did not seek alternate care for their child? This was clearly a case of a child being ill too often. Even though we sent him home consistently (many times upon arrival), the other children had a great increase in their illnesses during this period of time.

It is the center's responsibility to maintain standards of hygiene and keep sick children out of the center. You have a right to expect this and should not accept anything less.

It is also you—the parents—who are responsible for keeping your children home when they are not well. We expect the little runny noses and slight colds in group care. But when a child is visibly ill, even without fever, there is only one place for them to feel good and safe and get the rest and attention they need: at home with a parent.

A toddler confessed to us one morning, "Mommy took my temperature, she said if I take the purple medicine my fever will go away and I'll feel better." Even if your baby or toddler is preverbal, and there are not many chances he'll spill the beans, getting his fever down just to get him into child care for the day is just wrong. (This is an occurrence I am told is more common than I am able to uncover.) The child who is ill is at risk, as are all of the other children he comes in contact with.

There are unfortunately too many employers who are not sympathetic and understanding to an employee's need to take time for a sick child. This motivates otherwise responsible parents to put their children at what they are hoping is a minimal health risk. Jobs that offer telecommuting have helped parents, but unfortunately, these positions are in the minority.

As working parents, it becomes challenging to find time to devote to our children, and only our children. Typically we are juggling the many responsibilities of running errands, preparing meals, doing household chores, working at the computer at home, and talking on the phone. Being at home with a mildly ill child is a good excuse to forget all of that, and just cuddle reading stories, trying to help our little one feel better.

Toddlers in Child Care

The toddlers at this center are not challenged with a wide-open expanse that lures them to come and run through. Rather, furniture is positioned to offer cozy opportunities for them to engage in meaningful play:

- Water play is readily available and offered daily.

- Art is a sensory experience and child-directed. (No prefab cookie-cutter teacher-made cutouts!) Materials such as clay, paper, crayons, paste, are easy to access.

- Tables and chairs are perfectly toddler-sized and allow for small group interaction of four to six children.

- Music is integrated as a soothing background, to ease a transition, or inspire a creative expression of movement and song.

- Books and stories are readily available, maybe in a cozy corner of the room, where there is a couch or other soft furnishings to relax in. Many ethnic groups are represented in picture books about familiar experiences.

- Housekeeping and dress-up captivate toddlers as they mimic real life. They are acting out meal preparations, family situations, and much creative play that keeps them absorbed.

- Large muscles are exercised with various climbing and crawling opportunities.

- Puzzles and manipulative toys are in good condition and aid fine motor definition as young hands develop. Labels with pictures to indicate where toys and materials belong line the shelves.

- A block area encourages imagination, allowing children to build representations of their ideas and fostering cooperation and social skills. Blocks are large and hollow or soft to facilitate usage. Miniature people, animals, and transportation vehicles aid in the creative play.

The Staff

When we visit the toddler room, we're not surprised to find these growing children testing limits. The adults in the room do not receive this with exasperation, anger, or excessive "No's." Power struggles with this age group are avoided because these toddlers are offered choices that are safe and suitable. Caregivers gently direct behavior with positive words. Routines are organized so waiting is minimal. Toddlers are not expected to sit or to all join in a group activity. Sharing is not a must or even a goal. There are options for children to choose from throughout their day. Caregivers are flexible in their routines, thereby

---

Red Light Warning

Toys are up high on shelves, in children's view but beyond their reach. Staff are continually picking toys off the floor to keep the room tidy.

---

responding to the individual needs of the children. Positive self-esteem is the result of toddlers being encouraged to search for solutions to everyday dilemmas, such as putting on a shoe, looking for a lost toy, or fitting a puzzle with the right piece. Open-ended questions and comments encourage children's persistence. Adults play with the toddlers and follow their lead in play. Stories, songs, and finger-plays are frequent, informal occurrences in this room.

Building upon exploration and discovery, social competence, and intellectual development are the goals that are set, and results are achieved when all is in place.

Group Care: The Ripple Effect

Or otherwise known as picking up the neighbor's bad habits! We all cringe at the thought of our innocent little *cherubs* coming home reciting slang words and phrases that are better left to the street. For the most part, the majority of these children have not a clue as to what these words mean. But they do know it gets the attention of the adults in the room, and some pretty bizarre reactions from them!

"Mommy you are a poo-poo head!" recited one toddler. Her mom came to me most anxious and annoyed at this display of behavior and apparent lack of respect from her daughter. "She never heard that expression at home, and certainly has never spoken to me like that before she started the center! What are you going to do about the child teaching these things to the class?"

The reality is, I know I am not the first director to hear these worries from a parent. It is not unusual for older children to bring this type

Red Light Warning

A staff member responding to a toddler's use of choice words with "Where did you hear that language? That's terrible! I am going to tell your mother!"

of conversation home (and unfortunately more vulgar language than that!) and for younger siblings to pick it up, thinking it very *cool* as well. Of course, these younger siblings then bring this new vocabulary to their child care setting.

Certainly, advise your child's teacher and/or the director when this occurs. Chances are pretty good they know where this is coming from and may already be addressing it. We do not, however, want to give the child displaying this behavior a lot of attention. Instead we will try to ignore the remarks, and if persisted, say very firmly, "These are not nice words, please choose others." Or, "When you use these words, I am uncomfortable, please choose other words."

As teachers and administrators we like to think we've heard it all. That is, until one day when you realize you haven't. This happened in our toddler class one day, and had I not been witness to it, I might not have believed it:

The children had just come into the classroom from the outside. They had a wonderful walk outside, and were getting ready to have their lunch. Amid coat hanging and hand washing, out of the blue, our toddler teacher was startled by the voice coming from behind her: "Hey *Bitch,* get over here!" Those words came from the mouth of a two-year-old boy addressing himself to her. Her eyes popped as her mouth dropped. She composed herself quickly, told him not to speak to her with those words, and quickly changed the subject. This two-year-old really had no idea what he was saying. But it was obvious he had heard this prior, most likely at home, and often enough to repeat it in the child care setting.

The more validity we give children choosing to shock us with their choice of words, the more fun they seem to have using them! So after you put your ears back in your head after an unexpected statement or word, take a deep breath, keep a straight face, and try not to give it too much merit. The more credibility the behavior gets, the more it will be perpetuated.

Bringing Toys from Home

Special things from home can be of great comfort to many children in a child care setting: a special blanket, a picture of Mom and Dad, or a special soft toy to cuddle with during rest time. These comforts help ease separation difficulties and can provide the security that many children find necessary.

> The more validity we give children choosing to shock us with their choice of words, the more fun they seem to have using them!

Parents and centers should try to limit objects from home to items similar to those just mentioned. Hero figures like Power Rangers, Batman, and battery-operated toys cause a great disturbance in the classroom and pose a potentially large safety hazard. There are those mornings, however, when separating your child from these favorites may be most difficult. In an attempt to avoid a power struggle, especially as you are trying to get everything organized and get to work in the morning, here are some suggestions to try:

- Ask your child check it into their cubby upon arrival, not to be removed until departure at the end of the day.

- See if your child's teacher will put it away, maybe in a special, "Toys from Home" basket, until the end of the day.

- Make your child a partner in this by letting her know the rules, and perhaps offering several choices so that she may decide where to put her toy for the day.

My oldest daughter Andrea was close to two years old. We were in the kitchen; I was standing facing the sink preparing dinner, and she was on the floor playing with all the pots in the cabinet in front of her. We were happily singing a song together, as we each went about our business, but really enjoying the moment and each other's company. Andrea got up from her spot by the cabinet and came to hug me from behind. It was a most endearing hug, one that said, "I love you. I'm having fun. Thank you!" All of a sudden, her hug from behind turned into a huge bite! Ouch! I literally had to pry her teeth off of me. Her appreciation and affection for our fun was more than she could express verbally, so she resorted to the only method she could summon up quickly.

Addressing Toddler Behavior

The ages one- to three-years-old bring many joys and challenges. It is a whole new world! We watch as our children are learning and doing something new each and every day. New skills are being acquired constantly. Each child is individual and will acquire new skills and interests when it is developmentally appropriate for that child.

Aggression

With all of the changes that are so rapidly occurring during these months, most children will experience some level of frustration. One child has a toy that another child wants. A child sees something in the store that he wants. Each child will deal with that frustration in a different manner. One child may throw a tantrum, another may throw an object! Some children will yell, yet others may hit or even bite. The language skills that are needed to express their thoughts may not be available to them in a moment of excitement. It is for that reason that until a child is not only articulate in expressing himself, but in control of his emotions, that he will resort to these types of behaviors.

Red Light Warning

Teacher's response to a biter: "You need to sit here in the corner by yourself to think about what you did!"

When they reach high levels of excitement and happiness, it becomes common for these children to express themselves in an unacceptable manner, like biting. When the class is dancing to fun music, or when a friend is playing a fun game with them, their excitement goes beyond what they can verbally express.

Biting is one topic that gets most parents very concerned. Unfortunately, biting is just the vehicle that an individual child is resorting to. It does not make any child a *bad* child or their parents irresponsible. It is, however, a frightening and potentially hazardous act. When the skin is broken, we worry about the exchange of germs from the biter to the bitten. If the bite is on the face, parents are concerned about scarring.

Because these instances are not premeditated but spur of the moment, the response from the adults must take that into consideration. Reactions to biting and other acts of aggression should be consistent. Children must firmly be told this is unacceptable: "Biting, (hitting, pushing, etc.) is not a choice." Or, "I don't like when you hurt your friends." "You need to use your words." Or, "What do we use our teeth (hands) for?"

The child who committed the act of aggression could assist in giving "first aid" (ice pack, etc.) and then be redirected into another area. Attention should be given to the child who got hurt. The hurt child is then encouraged to use his words. He benefits by telling the child who hurt him how that act made him feel. "I don't like that," or, "You can't hurt me." This reminds the hurt child that he has the ability and the skills to take care of himself, and not to let anyone hurt him. It also builds self-confidence.

Parents of *both* children should be notified when an act of aggression such as biting occurs, and what steps are being taken. Some centers do not agree with me on this, and feel the parents of the biter need not be notified unless a *real problem* has already been established. I think a parent being informed about an established problem is less of a partner than if they are informed all along. The day-to-day slight shove or grab of a toy need not be reported, but is treated as common toddler behavior. Though biting is not unusual in group settings, for the parents of the bitten, it steps outside those boundaries of ordinary behavior. Neither parent should be told the name of the other child involved. Not only is there no purpose in this, but it can be disruptive. I actually have had a parent, after doing some investigation, approach a two-year-old child and yell at him, shaking a finger in his face, for hurting her child. You need to trust that the center is doing their best in handling the situation. If you can't trust the center, then you may be in the wrong place. When a child exhibits a recurring biting or other aggressive behavior problem, a staff member should be assigned to the child on a one-to-one basis, to protect the other children, until that behavior is outgrown. This could be anywhere from one to four months. Parents should be partners in the steps that are being taken, and informed on an ongoing basis. This provides for the consistency that's needed from both the center and the family. Maintaining anecdotal information about the child may assist in determining precipitating influences, who was involved, and other patterns we may not have noticed. If the aggressive behavior does not cease in a reasonable amount of time or number of occurrences (for each center that may be different), alternate care for the aggressive child must be found. These children could be welcomed back when they have acquired greater language skills or a little more maturity. Sadly, this is not always in the best interest of the aggressor, but the safety of the larger group must be the first concern of the center.

> Though biting is not unusual in group settings, for the parents of the bitten, it steps outside those boundaries of ordinary behavior.

If your child does exhibit aggressive behavior, have faith. Do not spend a lot of time discussing his behavior with him. This will only give the subject attention and credibility in his mind. If you should find that your child is the recipient of an aggressive behavior, please remember where it is coming from: another child. Not a monster. Keep the lines of communication open with the staff, to ensure that they are taking all precautions to protect your child and others.

Discipline

It wasn't until one of the parents from the center was *caught* at the supermarket, that she pleaded with us for help. Her two-year-old was throwing a tantrum in attempt to get to the candy aisle: screaming, throwing himself, and hitting his mother. After the initial embarrassment, she almost appeared relieved when she saw his caregiver there. "I take two Tylenol and do deep breathing exercises each week before I have to encounter the market. This isn't even the worst. I don't understand how he doesn't do this at the center! OK—sign me up for that class."

When I hung the sign at our center announcing a parenting retreat, featuring a full-day workshop on Parenting with Positive Discipline, it did not surprise me to see a waiting list for the class grew quickly. Learning and applying positive aspects of child guidance are the most requested forms of assistance parents seek me out for. As "No" and testing limits become favorites with young toddlers, parents and caregivers alike will experience frustration.

The term *discipline* may connote to some a negative or harsh response to a child's action. Instead, think of it as a positive way to influence and redirect children's behavior. It is not about punishment—for punishment relates to what the child should *not* do. Positive discipline fosters what the child *should* be doing. It is a natural consequence to actions, not a punitive penalty.

When parents ask me about our discipline policy, they usually appear shocked when I tell them I do not believe in the classic "Time Out." Most come to me with tales of sitting their child in a chair, preferably in a corner by themselves, when they do something wrong— one minute for every year of the child's age. Who came up with this stuff anyway? I believe this is not only humiliating to the child, but serves absolutely no purpose. I have yet to come across a one-, two-, or three-year-old who understands the connection between sitting on a chair in the corner alone and the undesirable act they just committed. Contrary, they feel embarrassed and usually outraged. Parents are under the misunderstanding that their child's eventual settling down is a positive result of this Time Out. Instead, what the child understands is that he or she will be accepted again, once they calm themselves down. But this does not have a connection to what they did wrong. In my opinion, any center practicing this type of discipline is lazy. It is easy to reprimand a child by saying, "Go sit in the Time Out chair." It takes more thought and creativity to provide for effective and positive discipline and natural consequences. The following are some guidelines for first *avoiding* some potential struggles.

- Anticipate the situation and provide advance notice of any changes: "When Daddy comes back we will be leaving for Grandma's." Or "We are only buying one box of cereal at the supermarket today."

- Present choices whenever possible: "Do you want to put away the paper or the glue?"

- Have consistent, understood rules, with reasons: "No hitting—that hurts our friends."

- Offer attention for appropriate behavior that lessens the chances of needing attention for attention sake through negative acts: "Daniel, I really liked the way you helped David find the puzzle pieces."

- Select toys that provide children with the experience of success rather than frustration.

- Substitute positive statements for negative ones or "No!:"
  - Instead of "Don't climb on the table," try "The table is for eating our meals on."
  - Instead of "Don't color at the dining room table," try "Color your paper over here."
  - Instead of "Don't walk with the juice," try "I'll hold your juice while you get your doll."

When Alternatives Backfire

My daughter Traci was just two years old. While I was packing kitchen boxes for our upcoming move, she and her older sister were playing in the next room. After twenty minutes of a little too much quiet, I became suspicious. I nearly died when I saw the entire wall of my hallway covered from top to bottom in every color magic marker imaginable! There was Traci standing on a chair, trying to color in the last bit of white space left on my wall. Her older sister was obliviously involved in her own play.

I attempted to have Traci help me wash the wall at first. But after having made a thorough analysis of the situation, I realized I needed to paint it. I told Traci she couldn't join her sister in play, she needed to sit with me and watch as I painted (three coats!). Maybe I should have suspected her glee, by the fact that she sat there, hands over mouth, fighting back her giggles. (I had to fight back my own as well.) I threw away every marker I could find, finally feeling safe.

The next morning, out of bed before me, somehow, some way, Traci found one lone brown marker and covered the same wall with it. She sat with the same giggle hiding face watching, as I once again, painted.

Moral of the story? Make sure the clean-up consequence is not a fun undertaking for your child!

- Save "*No!*" for when you really need it. It will carry much more weight than if it is being used all the time.

Some ideas for alternatives to Time Out or punitive punishment and natural consequences:

- Remove the child from the negative situation, and redirect her into another more positive one: "When you throw the blocks, you're telling me you don't want to play in the block area. If you need to throw something, you may join our friends throwing the balls."

- Take the child from the area of conflict and sit *with* him until he regains self control. This is especially important for a child who is hysterical or acting out.

- Separate what the child did from who she is. For example, "I don't like it when you hurt your friends," instead of "You are always picking on Jack, when are you ever going to stop?" Or, "When you talk while I read the story, no one can hear it," instead of, "You are always so noisy. If you can't be quiet, you'll have to leave."

- Have the child *fix* what he broke or ruined: "I'll help you wash off the paint you used all over your sister's toy." Or, "You need to rebuild Johnny's block tower that you knocked over."

Praise and Self-Image

One of our toddlers strolled into the class one morning with her mother. She was wearing a new raincoat, and held the bottom edges, pinkies outstretched, as if she were about to curtsy. The vinyl coat was purple and had pink-and-white "flower power" flowers from the '60s all over it. One of our newer staff members took the hint, and approached her most excited: "Tiffany, I love your new raincoat! Did you and Mommy just buy it? It's great!" Boasting, Tiffany replied, *"Yes, and I can twirl in it too, see?"* And Tiffany proceeded to twirl in her new raincoat.

At the art table, the teacher's assistant was sitting and talking to the children. All the children were making collages. Matthew's had the most collage materials glued to the paper. The assistant said, "Wow, this is wonderful Matthew, I love your picture." Instinctively three other children chimed in, "Do you like mine?"

In both of these examples, the children were receiving or looking for praise that was not about them personally. We are so wrapped up in thinking our children's self-esteem and positive intrinsic values are directly linked to making them feel good with words of praise and encouragement. Praise and encouragement are only effective when they are real and not overused. When praise is random and global, it has no particular meaning to the child. When it is used excessively it loses its value. And when it is based on comparisons, it sets the child up for competition with others, not herself. Maybe the first teacher could have said; "Tiffany, it seems like you and Mom must have searched a long time to find such a special raincoat!" And perhaps Matthew's teacher might have noticed, "I see you working very hard to put so many pieces on your paper."

Express praise sincerely, on specific aspects of the child's achievements. "Valerie, you and Billy used a lot of care to build the blocks so tall!" Invite children to value the pains they put forth. "Lynda, I can see how much effort you are putting into your painting! You took a lot of time choosing the right sponges to dip in the paint." Provide approval for desirable behaviors. "I know how hard it was for you to share the trucks with Steven. I can see he is enjoying playing with you."

Let children's accomplishments be for their personal satisfaction, not to please a parent or teacher or to win a contest. Allow your praise of your child to be meaningful, not judgmental based on what you or the teacher might determine to be acceptable. Something that reminds him he has thought well, has contributed great effort, or has done something of particular value. Building our children's self-image is a priority we all share as parents and early childhood educators. We want our children to feel confident in the decisions they make and have the courage to take the risk of failing with the knowledge that they are still worthwhile. The partnership between parents and the center should work toward that together. With such an important goal for our children, isn't it worth taking the time to be discriminative in how we praise? Let's build our children's images of themselves by giving them respect, support, and high expectations, specific to their goals and accomplishments.

Sharing

"It's mine!"

"No it's mine!"

Sound familiar? I don't know any parent or caregiver of one- to three-year-olds who has not witnessed this struggle.

Toddler's Creed

If I want it, it's mine.

If I give it to you and change my mind later, it's mine.

If I can take it away from you, it's mine.

If I had it a little while ago, it's mine.

If it's mine, it will never belong to anybody else, no matter what.

If we are building something together, all the pieces are mine.

If it looks just like mine, it is mine.

—Author Unknown

Let's face it. No matter how we think we can effect the behavior of these young toddlers regarding right and wrong and sharing, we cannot. These children are not ready to share, and should not be required to. Learning to share is a process that takes time. Young toddlers are just discovering themselves. At two years old they are becoming more independent and autonomous. Things that belong to them are reminders of their own identity. When in a group setting, the expectation of sharing is like having to offer up a piece of themselves! Then, if they do offer that piece, who knows—maybe they won't get it back! Give and take with others is a new social experience. Toddlers see the world from only their viewpoint. They do not consider each other's needs before they are three years old. Then, even at three, this perception of others is just beginning.

Ideally, toys and materials in the toddler's room are presented without having to be shared. There is an ample selection of similar types of toy available. Several of the same colors of crayons and paints are accessible in the art area.

The layout of the room is conducive to only a few children participating at one time in a particular area. If the water table has room for four children around it, then four of the same kinds of water toys are available to the children.

Socializing

The unpredictable nature of toddlers can make socializing almost impossible. In fact, *friendships* are not a natural phenomenon to the toddler years, but are an inevitable result of group care. Though toddlers instinctively recognize *one of their own,* they do not have the skills

Red Light Warning

A teacher or caregiver telling a young child: "You need to share!"

to make friends. A nudge or a pat may frequently be their manner for making contact with other children. A toy may only become enticing when in the arms of another. That's when the "Toddler's Creed" comes to life. And so does potential biting, hitting, and yelling.

As these young children approach two years old, they enjoy watching and copying other children's actions. Small group size will facilitate their ability to make friends, as they begin to feel safe. As interactions become part of a regular routine, strong relationships are formed.

Potty Readiness

Potty readiness has been known to cause a lot of parents anxiety. In many cases, it has earned its reputation justly! Though a center may have their own "potty training policy," I would hope that it would include a partnership with the parents, and developmentally appropriate goals for each child individually. These suggestions for surviving the potty years can only be valuable if both parents and caregivers are practicing alike and maintaining consistent communication.

For starters, there's readiness. How will you know if your child is truly ready to embark on this journey? If you start too early (prior to eighteen months to two years), she may not be totally successful for a much longer period of time. There are three key facets to determining her readiness.

1. **Physical:** Your child has the physical ability to control his bladder and bowels. He or she wakes up dry from naps, and maybe even at nighttime. She will possibly find a corner to crouch in or a table to hide under when she is having a bowel movement.

2. **Intellectual:** Your child knows what the toilet and potty are for, and can relate this to herself. She possesses the verbal skills needed to communicate her needs.
3. **Emotional:** Your child wants to do this. She is motivated. "No" is no longer her favorite word. This is probably the one a lot of parents get stuck on. I'll address some of these obstacles a little later.

Once **all** three key facets are present, the following list of do's and don'ts will aid in your child's success. Remember, consistency and maintaining strong communication with your child's teacher will be the road to your child's success.

Do:

- Praise your child when she is successful.

- Limit fluids; substitute water for juice.

- Be prepared for plenty of accidents.

- Encourage your child.

- Treat accidents matter-of-factly.

- Remember, *old habits die hard;* have patience.

- Take your child to the bathroom frequently, and be prepared to sit. Have some books handy!

- Have your child assist in cleaning up his accidents.

- Dress your child in easy pull-up clothing.

- Let your child watch same-sex family members in the bathroom.

- Have little boys sit down at first to urinate.

Don't:

- Scold your child for having accidents.

- Be tempted by books or articles that promise *toilet training in a day!* This is a process, not an event.

Red Light Warning

A teacher or caregiver saying to a child: "You know better than to have an accident. I am very disappointed in you!"

- Bribe your child to stay dry.

- Compare your child to another.

- Put your child in clothing that is difficult for them to remove themselves.

- Offer rewards such as candy for success.

- Go back and forth from underwear to diapers or use the pull-on version of diapers as a guise for progression to underwear. This sends mixed messages. The pull-on version of diapers can actually reverse potty progress, as soiling in these does not feel so uncomfortable as to motivate the child to use the bathroom instead.

Obstacles

- Many children will show signs of readiness at home first and not at all at school, or vice versa. This is normal. Let your child's teacher know what is happening at home; share information. Continue to encourage success, and it will happen.

- Frequent accidents can discourage the most seasoned of parents. Don't despair! If your child truly has the three points of readiness, it will pass. It may take two to three weeks of accidents before habits begin to change, though. If you lose faith in your child, so will she. If you react with anger or exasperation, rather than matter-of-factly, you will build your child's anxiety on the subject.

- Being the "baby" can be rewarding for many children. Holding on to the diaper can be a control method of holding on to their babyhood. Don't make this a power struggle between you. If a new baby is in the home, or the family has recently moved, your child's security is threatened. This may not be the best time to initiate the process.

- If however, you and your child's teacher feel that your child is very ready, there are no threatening changes in the home, but your child does not want to give up the diapers, here are some ideas. . . .

  – Have your child assist you in bringing her diapers to a family with a *baby*.

  – Have your child choose the purchase of special big girl or boy underwear.

  – Put up a special sticker chart that your child gets to see and use only when in the bathroom.

  – Have several favorite books in the bathroom along with a potty book for further inducement. (My personal favorite is *Once Upon a Potty* by Alona Frankel.)

  – Spend some time in the bathroom with your child fully clothed sitting on the toilet or potty. Remember, it is important that your child "buys in" to this new endeavor.

Nighttime control does take a bit longer than daytime. When your child is waking up most mornings dry, it's time to take the plunge into underwear at night, maybe with a training pant over it. Protect bedding with waterproof pads under the sheet, and try some heavy sheet towels wrapped over the sheet midway down the bed. When accidents occur at night (and they most likely will), you will only have to change your child and remove the towels.

Lastly, remember your child will not go to kindergarten in diapers! A lot of patience and great sense of humor will see you through this stage unscathed.

Language Development

My oldest child, Andrea, spoke her first word at eight months. She spoke three-word sentences at twelve months, and by eighteen months, was able to have a complete conversation with an adult. My second child, Traci, did not speak an intelligible word until she was two years old. And my son Michael went the textbook route, somewhere in the middle. All are bright and articulate, but are programmed very differently. I have always said, "My husband and I have given birth to three different children, who appear to have three different sets of parents!" I pull that story out each year as parents come to me concerned because their eighteen-month-old is not speaking at the same rate as another. Though I believe each child is programmed to develop language at the rate that is right for them, external factors do influence this rate.

> Learning to share is a process that takes time.

- The firstborn children in the family tend to speak earlier than their siblings. Why? Parents devote all of their available time to number one. They speak to him directly and with frequency. He gets all of their attention, without having to share them. We know that the more babies are spoken to, read to, and exposed to language, the more they will pick up. The new studies on infant brain development prove (what we knew all along!) the physiological benefits to brain growth and intelligence. But not all children will perform according to the same time clock.

- Second children or the "baby" usually lean to one extreme or the other. Either their needs are so anticipated by older siblings and parents that the need for them to speak is not paramount, or they want to be included in the older siblings world and pick up their language very early.

As long as your child's developmental language milestones are progressing without concern from your pediatrician, there should be no need for worry. Ask the questions of your pediatrician if your child:

- Has had chronic ear infections prior to two years old. Fluid in the ear could have contributed to hearing loss and subsequent loss of proper language development.

- Was adopted from a foreign country where the history of medical and nurtured care is not known.

By eighteen months old, young toddlers are searching hard for the words they need to express their thoughts. They understand far more than they can articulate. The frustration level begins and will not taper until the toddler has some mastery of his language, somewhere between two and three years old. Have you ever listened in on a conversation between a couple of two-year-olds? It is an endearing experience, and one that can give you insight into their ability for verbal expression.

Encounters such as vacations or a new school, home, or sibling are natural inducements for spurring language growth. After all, new adventures stimulate fresh thoughts and questions. Those thoughts have a need to be shared, and language is the perfect conduit! Watch those teachers who take the time to talk, play, and sing one-on-one with the children. They are creating openings for developing communication. These adults also know to be patient as they anticipate a toddler's response. As your toddler becomes more and more proficient in his ability to converse with others, you will appreciate the budding preschooler he is now becoming.

7

The Endurance

Preschoolers

She's out of diapers, and tells you a bottle is for babies. Peanut butter sandwiches for lunch are preferred to the warmed-up veggies she used to beg for. She uses words like *actually* and *perhaps,* and (hooray!) the word "Yes" has reentered her vocabulary! The dimples in her elbows and knees are decreasing almost before your eyes, and she wants to know how the baby in the Mommy's belly is going to get out. Her toddler years are quickly blossoming into her preschool years.

Just when you think your *terrific two*-year-old has taken the *terrific* out of it, the *thankful threes* appear. What a joyous age three starts out as! Cuddly and lovable, *threes like to please.* They engage in cooperative play with other children, and turn taking and sharing start to have meaning. So do friends. They are kind and sensitive to their friends until the more bold and aggressive behavior of the *fours* emerges.

Self-help skills are a reality and a need for the preschooler, as a newfound proficiency is a reminder of maturing abilities. Temptations call you to hurry her up because you can do something quicker and better, but your patience becomes a handy adult attribute; you don't want to discourage her persistence at the task. She may be showing an interest in letters and numbers, and can recognize her name in print. And you're amazed at her growing capacity to sit for a longer duration!

So how do all of these changes affect her life at the child care center? How can parents and centers together support her changing needs? Second to leaving an infant, the most difficult transition parents make in child care is the post-toddler transition. Not because Mom or Dad cannot leave their three-year-old; quite contrary, most are delighted to leave them at this age! The fear of the unknown is much less, because their child can talk. She can report the good, the bad, and the ugly! This transition becomes difficult because the apron strings need loosening from both ends, and realistic goals for each individual child must be agreed upon. Parents' needs may be wrongly assumed to be much fewer, just because their children's now are, as compared to the infant and toddler years.

Communication and Information Sharing

Each center has its own unique systems for reporting information to parents. We hope to find a page or notebook with a written daily record for infants and toddlers. But what happens when baby is past those toddling years? Should parents be given the same daily exchange of information? Are they automatically to stop caring about things their children have done, like "How much of their meal did they eat? Who did they play with? Who did they argue with? What programming engaged them that day? Did they join in the group activities? How was their mood? Did they sleep at rest time? How many times did they go to the bathroom? How long did they cry after Mom left that morning?"

Naturally, as parents we want as much information about our children as is possible! But the reality is, as our children begin maturing, the need for much of this knowledge declines. And so does the availability of the staff to provide it daily! Following are a few guidelines for when you should be receiving communication from the preschool center's staff.

A little note to tell you . . .

- It was an especially wonderful day for your child. Maybe he was able to do something that was previously too demanding or challenging. Shared a beloved toy, built a tall block tower, participated in an activity, or perhaps just cleaned up his own spilled yogurt!

- Your child gets an injury. If it is more than a scrape on the knee, a phone call in addition to a written report of the incident is appropriate, especially if the injury is on the face. You don't want to walk in at the end of a long day and be surprised noticing your favorite smiling face wearing a big red scratch mark! This note does not need to tell you who the offending child is, but rather what the circumstances of the injury were, what first aid (if any) was administered, and what your child's reaction was. I always train our staff to report the facts only, not to make inferences or judgments about the incident.

- Your child's behavior has been a problem. We call this the *uh-oh notice.* (Our euphemism for it: "just to let you know.") You know the one—your child bit, hurt, or acted out. I hope this type of notice is not coming home arbitrarily for every shove or upset. A normal amount of daily pushing or noncompliance is expected. If notes go home about each of them, it really is putting a disproportionate amount of attention on the matter. These situations should be handled in the class, with no need to go further with them. The note should be saved for when a problem is beginning and parents need to be kept abreast of the situation, or if their child caused more than a light injury to another.

- A child is struggling with a specific problem. Continual contact between parents and teachers would also be critical in this situation. A daily journal could be exchanged in the hope of understanding and resolving the concern. Patterns may be noticed from these ongoing reports, and consistent responses at home and at the center would be established.

- Your child is having a sleeping problem. A paper with the question, "Who napped today?" could be placed by the sign-in sheet with each child's name on it and a check mark next to their name indicating whether they slept or not during rest time.

It is wonderful when teachers can share some of their activities and happenings in the class with the parents, outside of the obligatory monthly calendar. Our teachers love to do a synopsis of a week's fun for the parents in a short letter. Sometimes the day is so exciting they will leave a letter for the parents the same day! Many cooking projects are shared when the teacher leaves the recipe for the parents. Songs and finger-plays make their way home just by having teachers make copies of them for parents. If your center is not getting the news of these fun stories and projects to you, ask them about it. They might be very willing to put a small informal weekly letter together, or copies of a new song, just for the parents of your class. Having this information at your fingertips is great for getting your preschool child to open up to you. Instead of the usual response of "I don't know" to your daily "What did you do today?" you are now armed with terrific insider info and can ask leading questions: "What did you find on your nature walk today? Who got to crack the eggs for the muffins you baked? Which part of the "mittens" story do you think was silliest?"

When information coming home had been lagging with my own children, I tried asking questions like "What was the messiest thing you did today? The funniest? The hardest?" These kinds of questions squelch children's never-ending desire to describe their day globally by telling us they did *nothing* or they *just played*. How rewarding it is to be able to talk with your child about their day, knowing that you did get to share in it, even if just a little bit. Your child will also appreciate having you as a *participant* in their recollections of their time in the center.

Photographs

Imagine this: walking in at the end of the day, and seeing a large poster board filled with pictures of the children in your child's class—an illustrative testament to their fun-filled week. There is your darling, having fun, looking interested, playing, and laughing! (You were secretly convinced she moped and sat at the table alone all day!) Seeing your child joyfully engaged through pictures is worth more than any other kind of communication. Many centers will document the children's day with cameras, keeping the pictures posted for all to see.

Three-year-old Andrew did not have a positive experience at his previous center. His mom prepared us for the worst. "He will sit in a chair and scream, maybe an hour or two. They couldn't do anything to make our good-byes any easier. So I finally gave up. When I would call later, he would still be upset, maybe not hysterical or anything, but definitely unhappy. They did try, really they did, but he was always crying. He would never participate or do anything the other kids were doing. So I know you'll have a tough beginning with him, but hopefully this new environment will eventually make a difference."

After his mom left, Andrew did cry. Our staff started to do their *thing,* which ends up being a combination of empathy and distractions to help the separating child. Though many staff and children approached him, Andrew preferred to sit quietly in a chair, not wanting to be touched or disturbed most of the morning. But by ten o'clock, something happened. The teacher from his class came running in to my office, saying, "You have to come see this!"

I heard the sounds of happiness and music outside the room. I watched as the class became engaged in the fun and children began dancing. In the middle of this excitement was Andrew, on the first day of his new school, dancing! And laughing! And having a good time. Well, we couldn't wait to run and call Mom and tell her. She was thrilled, of course, but we sensed she really did not believe what we were telling her. (She later explained she thought we had exaggerated Andrew's exuberance, just a little!)

At the end of the day, Andrew's mom arrived to pick him up. You can imagine her joy being greeted by several pictures of a jubilant little boy (her son!) dancing with the other children. Those pictures made her day, and Andrew's. He carried them around for quite a while. If your child's class does not have a camera, consider making a gift of one to them! It is a wonderful vehicle for sharing special moments as well as daily routines. They can also help bridge the gap after the daily sheets home have ceased.

I have often felt as if the weaning of parents off their daily dose of infant/toddler information was a traumatic experience for many. One of our biggest issues as working parents is losing control of our children's days. These daily bits of communication gave us questions to ask, reasons to act, and generally provided for our continuing influence into their time away from us. As our children grow, and programs evolve, so must we. Satisfying our need to have influence into their daily experiences can still be fulfilled, but may take some reevaluating of our priorities and our children's needs.

Supporting Your Child's Changing Needs

The continuum of development during these preschool times means teachers and parents regularly must look to reassess their expectations of the children. Adults may become trapped into anticipating too much independence and maturity from them, or not enough. Opportunities for children to practice their self-help skills should be provided with patience and understanding.

Many three- and four-year-olds desperately require a daily nap. Then there are those who gave up their nap at two and couldn't sleep during the day if their life depended on it. Some preschoolers crave space and movement, while others hunger only to read and write. We have all witnessed those children possessing a talent for imaginative play that is captivating, but some of their peers may not know how to join them. How can a center be all things to all of their children? Though not always attainable, I believe a center does have a responsibility to attempt just that.

Four-year-old Molly was a *bear* by supper time if she hadn't had at least a one and a half-hour nap each day. Sadly for Molly and her parents, the dynamics of the children in that class were such that nap time was a joke. Sure the classical music went on, lights went out, and the teacher in the room read a story to get everyone in the mood, but this group would have none of it. They chatted, sang, laughed, strolled around the room, and made at least six trips to the bathroom and water fountain each. It got to the point that the teacher ended up engaging in a power struggle attempting to get these children to sleep. We had complaints from Molly's parents, who needed her to sleep, and complaints from other parents that their children were required to stay on a mat and be quiet. As we became aware of the challenges facing this class, we knew we needed to make some changes. We first changed the lunch hour of the staff member with whom the children were struggling. She would no longer be responsible for transitioning the children into this quiet time. We

> Opportunities for children to practice their self-help skills should be provided with patience and understanding.

then determined that except for Molly, this class does not need to sleep! But they could all use a little rest and down time. So we changed our format for this class. Lights went out, classical music went on, and children still needed to have their mats set up. But everything else changed. Tables in the room were each set up with different quiet activities for the children to engage in: puzzles, books, writing, simple art, board games, computer time, and the listening station with stories on tape through headphones. Talking was permitted, but soft voices only. Some children even chose to rest on their mats, knowing they could sing to themselves in a quiet tone and it would be OK. Unfortunately for Molly, this was still too much stimulation for her, and she was unable to sleep in this environment. But she did happily agree to take her mat to another class where children were sleeping, and was able to get the sleep she needed.

Many systems for daily routines are most likely in place in your center, but it's the flexibility to respond to the group or the individual child that should not be overlooked. When this philosophy is accepted, meaningful and pertinent care for children can be provided. But remember it is the responsibility of both parents and the center to look with open eyes.

Clarence had recently turned three. He came to the center each day with a lunch box full of food. As a young toddler, he ravenously devoured these banquets. But his eating needs were changing, and more and more of his lunch was coming home. Mom became very concerned and began setting rules for Clarence during meal times. We did not want to contradict this parent's need to do what she believed was right for her child, yet enforcing any type of guidelines for food consumption was completely against the center's philosophy and practice. We explained our approach to children's changing appetites and why requirements for finishing meals were not part of it. This parent did not agree with us. She was able to affect her child's eating habits at home with her rules and believed we were just not being strict enough. As a compromise, we agreed to offer Clarence the balance of his lunch when he awoke from his nap, while maintaining our position of not being forceful and without mandating a quantity of food for him to eat.

> Many systems for daily routines are most likely in place in your center, but it's the flexibility to respond to the group or the individual child that should not be overlooked.

Of course, there will be occasions when the center and parents will not agree. Unless the safety and well-being of the child is a concern, or it is a direct contradiction of established center philosophy, I always believe that the parent's wishes must be followed. But we both have the obligation to make adjustments whenever possible to meet a child's changing needs. Frequent communication with the center should afford opportunities to be creative and supportive in an attempt to meet them.

Addressing Your Preschool Child's Behavior

We survey our parents twice yearly, to see how we're doing in their eyes. I can always count on several parents to bring up two concerns. The first is that they don't feel they are informed enough when their child *misbehaves*. The second is a request to offer more parenting workshops on discipline. I string these two issues together because they naturally link to children's conduct.

Strangely, parents seem to feel that if they are not receiving discipline notes from the center, they are not being told when their child has acted inappropriately. They find it difficult to accept that we may not be having the same concerns in the center as they do. It is not unusual for behavior to favor one extreme at home and another at school. Different circumstances, environments, and limitations all contribute to this. When parents finally share their thoughts, we hear a myriad of issues regarding their sudden inability to affect their child's behavior. Threes becoming fours will tend to be more aggressive, disagreeable, and seek attention through the use of four-letter words and other outrageous means. And those newly arrived threes may not live up to what may be the grander but inappropriate maturity standards some adults believe they should possess.

I hung a notice at the center announcing an upcoming parenting workshop on positive discipline. I thought it would be fun to entice parents with a flyer that had amusing questions on it, beckoning them to come find some answers at the class. Another parent thought it would be more comical to answer the flyer hanging in the entrance hall with his own solutions. I came in one morning to find the following responses added to my flyer hanging in the center.

What do you do when your darling three-year-old tries to strangle her baby sister? —Get out of the way.

How can you go to the mall with your kids, without intense counseling prior? —You can't.

> When we go to the market I will let you chose one thing for yourself.

How should you handle your child when he throws a tantrum at the supermarket because you won't buy him a balloon? —Buy him the balloon.

What do you do when your child insists on sleeping in your bed with you? —Roll over.

Though we all laughed at the responses written in with marker for all to see, this parent was saying something else too. He was giving up. Not having the right tools to positively redirect his children's behavior, he had lost a battle.

In chapter 6, "The Survival," I offer many strategies for positively influencing toddler behavior. Those ideas can also be applied to your growing preschooler. Consistency and giving our children clear messages lets them know what we expect from them. When limits are not explicit, children sense our ambiguity and naturally will seek to push those limits. Choosing our battles in advance can also arrest a potential dispute.

We want to have appropriate expectations for each child. Individual temperaments must be considered when choosing which techniques to implement. Not every child will respond the same way. Explanations for rules must be offered, and positive choices need to be given. Redirecting children can arrest challenging behavior, but maybe not as easily as it did during the toddler years. And natural consequences to negative actions will have even more significance.

Any response to our children's behavior must be logical if they are going to gain from it. Children do understand reasoning when it is kept simple, because it makes sense!

Naturally, with each passing month, old concepts will have new meaning. As small amounts of time go by, your child is experiencing new frontiers. He has a wider variety of interests outside of himself. His

Bats are for hitting balls with. You're telling me you are not ready to play with a bat when you keep swinging it around almost hitting people. This is the third time. We'll have to put it away and try again another day.

vocabulary has developed, and *using his words* is rarely something you need to remind him of. Testing limits may appear more deliberate, and socializing becomes a need, not an incidental fate of group care! Supporting your child during this growth period requires your continuing confidence in his ability to meet appropriate expectations.

As They Grow

When I was growing up, the philosophy was "Do as I say, not as I do," "A little fear goes a long way," and of course my favorite, "Children should be seen and not heard." Well, we certainly have learned a lot about parenting and children since then, and we know those sayings have no validity in current child care practice. Those theories were based on inappropriate expectations of how children learn and respond, and what they should be able to do.

Many programs place children in mixed-age groupings. This can be refreshing, as it exposes children to a wide range of abilities in a classroom. These kids can develop at a rate that is more natural and less competitive. It provides opportunities for nurturing and feelings of self-worth for the older children as they assist younger ones and become role models. For ease of staffing issues and licensing requirements, most facilities will group children by ages, milestones, and their schedules. It is not unusual for the adults (parents and caregivers) to expect more from a child who newly transitions to the *next class* in a center. This expectation may revolve around potty training, maturity

One of my teachers, newly out of college and mentoring under another more experienced teacher, came to me utterly exasperated after her first day with her new three-year-old class.

"Four children had accidents. Max had four accidents himself! Carrie took toys away from any child she even saw with one, and Jonathan just sucked on his thumb most of the day. Jennie kept hitting anybody who crossed her path, and I still cannot understand a single word Sammy says. Oh yes, only three of the sixteen children sat for more than a minute at the circle this morning! I thought these kids were all ready for preschool!"

It is obvious that this new teacher still had much to learn about the development of three-year-olds! But just as this teacher had unrealistic expectations for her class, so do too many parents.

levels, and cognitive or physical abilities. "He's not a toddler any more, he's in the preschool class!"

The Preschool Program

I get at least ten calls a day from parents researching child care options. I am always shocked to learn about the many misconceptions that still prevail about the types of education and care for children: "I want my child in preschool, not day care." Or, "Preschool is where they learn, right?" My usual private and silent response is *"I always thought children could not help but learn!"*

There was a time when *preschool* meant teachers were educated and a curriculum was in place. The antithesis was *day care*—where working parents left their children to be baby-sat by uneducated caregivers for long days. Though those unfortunate definitions are still out there, that is not the standard aspiration or general practice in early childhood education. Centers that are termed preschool only are most likely defining their hours as being part-time or serving the three to five preschool age group. Those termed as child care are probably representing themselves as having more full-time availability.

Each center or preschool will be different, and should be evaluated on its individual merits and how it meets your personal needs, not its classification.

Developmentally Appropriate Practice for Preschoolers

Toddler parents are usually forgiving when a program's philosophy is a *learning through play* one rather than an academic one. They're still babies! But then something happens when the child hits three; the competition becomes fierce as some parents want their child to be able to outperform the next one. There is still the misnomer that the smart children are those who can recite letters and numbers. I get at least one daily call or visit from a parent justifying how bright their young child is by telling me, "He can say his ABCs and 1, 2, 3s." There are *educators* (I use the term loosely) who still believe that *learning is a result of children who are doing paper and pencil seat work.* Programs that highlight these skills are developmentally inappropriate for young children. Though the children may learn to sound out or recognize words, they rarely understand what they are reading. Even sadder is that these children are at risk for losing their love of learning and school. Passivity sets in as teachers tell them what and how they should do. Those types of programs further complicate things by relying on improper evaluations to demonstrate what they believe the children have learned.

Statistics have been consistent in telling us that children in those types of programs do not do any better in school later on than those who have not been taught these skills during the early years. In fact, there is evidence to suggest that these children do not fare as well as those who have been in environments where play and opportunities *to do* were the prescribed philosophies.

Remember our DAP (developmentally appropriate practices) definition from chapter 2? Child-initiated and teacher-supported play still remain key components. Adults who have appropriate expectations become paramount, because children have such a wide range of maturation and physical adeptness in the preschool years. There are many different learning styles and interests within each group. It is not from flash cards that are drilled or ditto sheets that are traced that learning occurs, but from opportunities for hands-on experiences. Learning is not rote memorization, as some may have you believe, but an ongoing process of researching, questioning, discovering, understanding, and problem solving.

It is the whole child who is valued, and learning becomes a natural occurrence that supports the physical, emotional, social, and intellectual development of the children. Plain and simple, young children will learn by doing.

The Preschool Environment

Just as with babies and toddlers, the environment plays a critical role in the implementation of a developmentally responsive curriculum. Not enough choices in the room will result in bored children abusing any materials available to them. Too many random choices will peak confusion. But in our *ideal* setting, the chaos is organized and purposeful. Let's take a visit!

Unless the safety and well-being of the child is a concern, or it is a direct contradiction of established center philosophy, I always believe that the parent's wishes must be followed.

It certainly is difficult not to be enticed into this preschool room. Creative opportunities for children to research their surroundings are readily available. The adult-size sofa, abundance of plants, random quilts, and family pictures around the room remind you more of a living room than a classroom. No wonder you feel so welcome! Many activities are available for the children to choose among. Learning centers—small areas of interest in a room that are theme-based and have a physical definition—are set up, and the contents of these centers are changed with regularity to maintain interests. Wonderful possibilities for children to develop independence are overflowing here. There is no need to ask the adults in the room to get toys for the children, because the toys are all within a small arm's reach. So are the snacks! Since children's appetites are on different schedules, those who are in need of refreshments have the opportunity to help themselves. Those who are not can continue their play. There are signs that label the different spaces with words and pictures, telling children where things belong. This allows a sense of order and organization that permits respect for materials. It also begins to immerse our youngsters in a print-rich environment and provide for a link to the written word.

The "House" Center

Dramatic play and housekeeping areas have truly developed since the toddler years. There are many additions that lure young minds into expanding their play to include familiar work and family roles. This is always a favorite because it relates to topics that are central to a curriculum, and because it imitates daily life. It can become the grocery store, Laundromat, post office, hospital, work place, or any real situation. A wide variety of dress-up is irresistible, and these children can become anything. Dishes, dolls, and old infant seats are staples for imaginary fun. The child-sized kitchen is the cornerstone for all the culinary treats these kids can imagine! This space probably takes up a large portion of the room, as several children at a time will most likely choose to play here.

The Block Center

As you continue to look around, you're wondering why so much of the area has been dedicated to blocks of many different sizes and shapes. There are large wooden ones that are both hollow and solid, plastic blocks, and even small wooden blocks. And why are there trucks and figures of people included in this center? Is there a method to this apparently random selection of materials?

The block area learning center is the least understood by parents, yet it offers an incredible range of learning possibilities. Children begin by noticing the differences among each of the different blocks available: weight, size, shape, curves, and corners. Math concepts form as they begin to classify, count, and measure. Social development is assisted when, through children's cooperation skills, they are able to build and clean up side by side. They earn respect for each other's work by walking around another child's structure and not dismantling it with a kick. Figures of people are included in their pretend play. And did you know? Block building is a beginning for important reading skills. Shape recognition carries over to how children discriminate between letters and eventually words! And isn't it incredible that when children's ideas are represented through their block play, it is the same concept that's needed to represent their thoughts in written language? Just think of the science skills and spatial awareness needed to choose just the right blocks that will connect a bridge, balance a tower, or make a car go fast down a ramp. The dexterity and eye-hand coordination to make all these things happen are in bloom. So the next time you pass by the block area, take note: a lot more is going on here than most people realize.

The Art Center

When your eye is drawn to this next learning center, you realize your delight in having your child in this program. She would never have the opportunity to do in your home what these children are doing and thoroughly enjoying here. This messy art area is rarely unoccupied. There are materials that change with regularity. You probably see crayons, markers, paper of all different shapes and colors, varied collage pieces of assorted textures, glue, pencils, clay, scissors, magazines, and maybe each day something unusual and new to keep interests high. The easel has several colors of paints available and smocks hang nearby, so budding young artists are not at the mercy of staff to retrieve them out of a closet. A water or sand table might be filled with odd things of sensory value to the children such as shaving cream, goopy mixtures of teacher recipes, or just plain water with plenty of pouring and floating gadgets.

What really intrigues you about the art area is that attention is paid to these kids while they are enjoying the experience of their art, and does not necessarily focus on an end product. Children aren't rushed to *finish* their project. It is not about delivering a complete piece of work, but the process of doing it that is valued. Children are not asked what their picture is, but rather to narrate their picture so teachers can write their words on it for all to see and understand. Asking "What is it?" may be making an assumption that it *is* something, when the child may not want or have even thought of an identity for it. The room is a gallery dedicated to the display and celebration of the children's creative expression.

I will never forget the parent who, upon picking his son up at the end of the day, did not go to empty his Take Home folder. This folder in fact had not been emptied for at least a week or more. In protest, his son stopped him to show him his work that had accumulated.

"Daddy look at all the stuff I made!"

"What is this?" responded the rather disgusted father as he held up a piece of paper with paint all over it.

"I painted it."

"It's garbage. This is nothing." He then proceeded to crumple up the child's painting, throw it in the trash nearby, and drag his son out of the center.

I wanted to cry for the little boy, who was so excited about his painting. Sadly, his father did not put the same worth on it. This dad's reaction to his son's work was certainly not a typical parent response. But it always reminds me how precious our children's efforts truly are. When you take home and proudly display your child's art, it lets him know you appreciate his creation. Respond to his illustration with meaningful comments like: "I like the color red you chose, it makes me feel happy! . . . I see how you used the brush to make those lines. . . I can tell you worked very hard on this . . . It must have taken a long time to make so many dots . . . Tell me about your picture."

Art is a very personal thing, and each child will celebrate his work differently than the next. Celebrate with him!

The Manipulative Center

Now this next area you'll understand. It's filled with the kind of stuff you expected to find in the classroom. The manipulative area houses buckets or baskets of table toys including puzzles, peg boards, snap-together construction toys, stringing beads, and more. A table is nearby that facilitates use of these. Playing with and putting these little pieces together helps young hands develop, all in preparation for the finer writing skills they have yet to acquire.

The Reading Center

This is it—you've found it. You are in love with the quiet corner filled with the wonder of many intriguing books, which makes you want to curl up and spend your days here. There are soft furnishings, or hopefully an adult-sized sofa, with some comfortable pillows, and room for just a few children. It is set away from the noise of the busy block-builders and dramatic housekeepers to provide a place of calm and peace. Children can come and find refuge from the one main peril of group care: *There's always a kid in your face.*

Opportunities to develop language and literacy are readily available as is noted by poems, the children's dictated stories, and charts of the children's collective experiences hung around the room. At the writing table, children's own inventive spelling and writing paves the way for the skills they are in the process of developing. Paper, pencils, staplers, string, and hole punchers are also integrated here to encourage children's own bookmaking and imagination. Storytelling is an art practiced by the children as well as the teacher.

The Science Center

Your next discovery just begs for you to come and touch. The science table might host a variety of interactive materials for display as well as use. The class pet may reside here, as well as growing projects, magnifying glasses, scales for weights and measures, and the *catch* of the latest nature walk. It is an area that is always changing, growing, and captivating interests.

How the environment is arranged and stocked will not only influence the smooth running of the class but will also minimize conflicts. It will tell you what the teacher thinks is important by how much effort and space she gives each area. Your child will spend many hours here; how wonderful for you to be able to share and understand it!

Making Sense of the Curriculum

I have always been a believer that the best curriculum will fail in the wrong teacher's hands, but when in the right teacher's care, even a mediocre plan can be successful. The teacher sets the stage for children through an appropriate setting and expectations that allow for the individual needs, interests, and abilities. She is also sensitive to the many learning styles of the children she teaches, and designs the program to reach each of them, so all can experience success in this learning place.

> It is not from flash cards that are drilled or ditto sheets that are traced that learning occurs, but from opportunities for hands-on experiences.

This preschool teacher aims to create a balance of activities and opportunities that will meet the children's various developmental components.

Physical

Kids need to move! In the class setting as well as outside it. Teachers do not require children to be at tables and sit for any length of time. They are not only tolerant of children's movement around the class, but expect it! They have provided for this activity level with a responsive environment. Do you know how your preschool child's natural path through the living room seems to be over the couch and under the coffee table? She is discovering the limits of her body and how it relates to the external world. He instinctively knows how daily doses of gross motor play exercises his large muscles. You certainly want to see her get outside to relish climbing, crawling, and running to her heart's content. (Certainly more than in your living room!) Look to see ample opportunities for children to run and shout. They should be free to get their *yah yahs* out! (*Yah yahs* is a term I heard used by Carson's mom several years ago, and since fell in love with. It refers to that never-ending kid energy we adults always marvel at!)

Creative teachers will build meaningful activities of exploration and discovery into the outside environment as well. In addition to using large muscles, these kids are learning about the environment as they take nature walks, plant, and dig in the dirt.

Social-Emotional

Providing for the transition from toddlerhood to the threes, and then to the fours and fives requires a great understanding for what is a very broad spectrum of maturity and readiness. These teachers are displaying appropriate expectations for each child's abilities. For every child is celebrated for the special individual he or she is. Learning is associated with positive feelings because these kids are given the tools they need to thrive in this environment.

If I were to choose one reason why parents have expressed a love for child care centers, it would be their child's acquisition of social skills and emotional growth at the center. Where else can you find five four-year-olds sitting on the floor, all searching for pieces to a giant puzzle, asking meaningful questions of each other, passing pieces to a matching space, and discussing the possibilities. Where else will you see this same group sitting at a table, handing napkins, pouring milk, serving themselves, and chatting happily?

Your child is encouraged to solve her own problems, with assistance nearby if needed. She's asked open-ended questions to promote thinking skills, like: "How do you think this can be done?" "Is there another choice that would be fair?" "How else could you have done this?" Feelings and beliefs are validated by the teacher paraphrasing what she believes is responsible for the child's emotions. This not only confirms her understanding of his thoughts—"You're angry that Brice took the truck from you?"—it allows for the child to correct her: "No, I tripped over the truck!" It is this teacher's sensitivity to the children and their opportunities for cooperative interpersonal situations that facilitates their development of social and emotional growth.

Intellectual

You have probably noticed the children in this teacher's class working independently as well as in small groups. These sociable play/activities are rarely directed by the teacher, but are guided by her provision of appropriate materials that have meaning to the children's daily life.

Remember how each learning center becomes a backdrop for the skills that it enhances? Reading, writing, and music are also significant to this class because they are natural inclusions. Topics overflow and connect throughout the class space. These centers and activities have meaningful themes or topics such as animals, bugs, things that grow, feelings, family, weather, seasons, homes, cultures, transportation, people, the child herself, health, safety, community, and more. If bugs are the predominant month's theme, you may notice some changes and/or additions to the classroom.

Books about bugs will appear in the quiet corner. Large plastic creepy crawlers in baskets are now found by the block-building area to be incorporated into play. Posters of insects are newly hung in the room for motivation. There's a science table displaying an ant farm or similar habitat. Language charts have been hung, with the children's responses to descriptions of the bugs they saw on their nature walk, and assorted string and cotton have been added to the art area to entice children's fun and creative side of bug making.

> I have always been a believer that the best curriculum will fail in the wrong teacher's hands, but when in the right teacher's care, even a mediocre plan can be successful.

It is through this continuity and immersion into topics that the children *live them*. Being surrounded by so many facets of a theme gives their comprehension greater depth and meaning. It is relative to their everyday living. This multisensory approach allows the teacher to reach the many differing learning styles she encounters.

What also separates this class from others you have observed is the teacher's acceptance of different responses to her questions. She does not overly congratulate a right answer or condemn a wrong one. Instead she recognizes the validity of each and encourages the children's further exploration toward discovery. You won't see any ditto sheets or flash cards here. Rote memorization and isolated skill enhancement do not have roots in these children's lives.

As you begin to make sense of this curriculum and understand the program, you will appreciate each teacher's efforts with new respect.

How a topic relates to the lives of the children will become obvious. Adapting to meet the developing needs of your child becomes purposeful. And your partnership with the center will have been strengthened.

Let's Get Socialized!

My favorite times in the center are when I can sit in on a class and just watch. No note taking, no observing a *challenging* child we need to document behavior on, no teacher I must observe. I love to sit at one of the children's tables or on the floor with them and listen to their discussion, hoping I won't disrupt the conversation flow. What I hear sometimes reminds me of a group of older adults sitting at a table, playing cards! The children sound mature and grown-up discussing their meal, their parents, or their present activity. But there seems to be a bit of *con artist* in their attitude as well.

When they enter their third year, threes will choose to play independently as well as begin to enjoy cooperative play with small groups of other children. They can wait their turn for something, share, and even problem-solve their friend's dilemmas. Language is developing almost on a daily basis. This age will take great delight in role playing: "You be the baby, I'll be the daddy." But don't push them into groups. For some children at this age, being social can be very easy and comfortable, but others may still need more time. Don't forget that some of us are never truly comfortable in large social situations. Try not to project your own feelings of shyness or assertiveness, and allow for your child's natural gravitation to her own comfortable sociable level. You hope that her teachers will sense the red flags if this atmosphere becomes a truly painful one for her, and will share it with you. At that time you will be better able to strategize options for helping her.

Often, parents of toddlers moving into a preschool room will insist on placement of their child with another, their *best buddy.* Rather than make a demanding decision about who you want your child with in the next class, talk to the teacher. Many times what parents perceive as best friends and pairing at home may not be the same in the school situation. One child might overpower another, not allowing the first to come into his own. Other children may develop a love/hate relationship, where monitoring them becomes a full-time job for staff. There are those children who become dependent on each other and will not venture out to interact with others. And then to the surprise of parents, some children play well together at home, and even talk about each other, but will have little interaction during the school day. Discuss your child's friendships in the classroom setting with the teachers who spend the most class time with your child. They have the same goals and will want to place him with children he is comfortable with. Most centers will look to group the children by similar ages, racial balance for the class, boy/girl balance in the class, personalities, and the compatibility of children and their parents with a teacher. On the other hand, if placement into the next class is being tracked, meaning your center's grouping of children is the result of testing that determines academic or physical ability levels, you are in the wrong place. Run.

Aggressive Behavior

Those of you who have ever walked in to a group of four-year-olds might understand the anxiety many parents face. I think it's the shock of their child's sudden rambunctious, defiant behavior that jolts parents into a state of fear. They tremble with apprehension about the future destiny of their child! When these kids are emotionally overwhelmed, it's not unusual to see them resurrect the hitting, shoving, and yelling of their toddler days. One mom was so concerned over her son's turn-around behavior toward the aggressive side, she kept asking me if all the other children were afraid of him.

The brazen self-assuredness of this age can throw a wrench in what appeared to be smooth sailing in the discipline department. It is not unheard of for a four-year-old to express his anger with "I hate you!" Or "You're ugly!" This is also when bathroom talk and efforts to experiment and shock adults and other children are practiced with zest. Even *flashing* private parts of their anatomy seems like a good idea. They are fascinated with their sexuality and the differences between boys and girls. One mom was so distraught over her son's blatant interest in a little girl's body that she came to me contemplating several punishments (including no TV, dessert, or games). When we discussed the natural curiosity of four-year-olds and the benign origin of his inquisitiveness, she agreed that a simple but firm dialogue between them would suffice. Besides, none of those consequences were natural ones to the behavior she wanted to arrest. And did this behavior even warrant a consequence? Of course not; this boy needed an understanding of privacy and respect for other people's bodies as well as his own. Though it's certainly easy for parents to get excited about the subject matter, a simple discussion in which the child has the opportunity to feel safe and ask questions should be enough.

Sadly, physical punishment is still a vehicle used by many parents to *teach a lesson*. Its only results are the condoning of aggression by modeling it. I find most parents who have confessed to hitting their children do so because of their own lack of control over their emotions, not because the situation justified it. Parenting by force rarely earns respect and understanding, just fear. Use the undesirable incident as a teaching opportunity. Acknowledge your child's anger and disappointment: "I can see that you really wanted to play with that toy"; offer the rules or limitations that are in place: "but you are not allowed to take things from other children, and you are not allowed to throw the toys"; then offer him other solutions: "Maybe next time you can ask to play with the child using the toy, or wait until it is no longer being used." Once your child is aware of the rules in place, you can ask him what he could have done differently to solve his problem. Help him brainstorm. After all, how can we expect to assist our children's problem solving, if we cannot clearly identify our own means of problem solving?

Fours possess a new ability that provides for functioning on a more cooperative level. Though their behavior becomes more assertive, they will listen to reason and seek to resolve a difficulty with a peer. Their class experience should be a continuum of opportunities for them to develop successfully and nurture these social skills.

8

The Personal Side

Taking It Home

Your child care center is more than just the place where you drop your children off for the day. It is an environment you need to trust and to know intimately. You need to know that the people you leave your children with will care for them in a manner that represents your beliefs and desires. The center is an extension of your home, your work, and your life. The success of this new collaboration is not the result of an overnight event, but one that evolves with time and effort.

Parents As Partners

We hope that centers strive toward creating a partnership alongside the families for whom they care. Though some may still have a distance to go until that goal is reached, there are ways you can facilitate their progress. Rather than looking at just the center welcoming parents as a mode of accomplishing this (which they do need to do!), let's also talk about parents welcoming the center into their lives.

As parents, you are the first and most important teachers for each of your children. You possess the knowledge of your child's inherent nature and of your family's values. Communicating these will allow for your influence over your child's care in the center and will ensure both of your needs are met. A respectful alliance between the center and the family then becomes a collaborative means of caring for children. Without this partnership, security and comfort cannot truly be achieved.

Communicating your child's needs and educating her caregivers of your preferences allows for a greater understanding of your actions and for joint decisions to be made in the child's best interests.

Child care is a service-based business. Though we rarely think of parents and children as *customers* in a center, perhaps if we did, we would find care to be more representative of the families it serves. As a parent, you have a right to expect that your voice will be heard, and that centers will go out of their way to try to accommodate your needs. You would not want to contradict the program's philosophy or policies, but you should expect that the center will listen to you with respect and a willingness to try and understand and problem-solve *with* you. That doesn't mean that the center will agree to stay open an hour later one evening for a parent who needs to work late; that your child's out-of-town cousin will be allowed to come to child care with her for the day; or that a center will follow through with a parent's request to use physical force on their child to *make them listen.* (I have had all of these requests from parents.) However, it does provide for you to have influence over how your child is treated during the course of a day. After all, when we leave our children in child care, we are not abandoning our parental rights for those nine hours, nor are we relinquishing our visions of what we want for them. Child care is not a surrogate parent, and contrary to the beliefs of the critics of dual-working parent families, these children are not being *raised* by their caregivers.

> As parents, you are the first and most important teachers for each of your children. You possess the knowledge of your child's inherent nature and of your family's values.

Feeling Resentful of Your Child's Caregiver

I'll never forget the first time I was asked by an expectant mom, "Don't the babies end up loving the caregivers more than their parents? I mean, they spend more time with them than the parents do."

It is natural to feel insecure about this new relationship. For some it may occur exclusively when their baby is very young; for others it may continue for the length of their child's days in care outside of the home.

Parents of young babies suffer the most with these feelings of jealousy. There are so many uncertainties about this new life that they are discovering. The physical demands of being a new parent are more debilitating than originally bargained for. The ambivalence of returning to the workforce has not been reconciled yet, and they have not figured out who this little person is, and what all of his needs are. Then, just as things begin to make sense, the bottom of the laundry pile is in sight, baby is sleeping through the night on a fairly regular schedule, and his personality is charming and captivating—it's back to work. Somehow it does not seem quite fair.

Babies and children inherently know the difference between parents and caregivers, even if the amount of wake-time spent with each is lopsided. The unconditional love and bond between a parent and his child will not be severed because additional bonds are being formed. Those additional attachments actually give children reasons to trust more as their parents provide for their time away from them.

The mom of one of our three-year-olds was devastated at the difficult time she had persuading her daughter to leave at the end of the day. It was late, but several of the children, including hers, were building a super-highway connecting the block corner to the housekeeping area with Ms. Kirbee. After five minutes of Mom's cajoling and attempting to pry Mara away from the activity, Mara looked up at her mom and announced: "I don't want to go home. I want to stay with Ms. Kirbee!"

When children are tired at the end of the day, or involved in something, making that transition back to parents and home life can be challenging. Imagine that you are deeply engrossed in a project at

> Child care is not a surrogate parent, and contrary to the beliefs of the critics of dual-working parent families, these children are not being *raised* by their caregivers.

work, one that you had been working on for a long time with your coworkers, and was very proud of. Then imagine your spouse entering the scene attempting to coerce you away from it, just as you are about to test the project's worthiness. You might not be inclined to want to leave, and it could appear that you prefer the company of your coworkers! Naturally, of course, that is not the case, but translate that scenario to your child's world, and you might understand some of her reluctance to leave.

Though we all would like to envision our babies and children leaping out of the caregiver's arms to get into ours upon immediate sight, not all children will. Would we sacrifice our child's happiness while away from us for that? I don't think so. We want our children to be with individuals who are nurturing, caring, fun, and understanding. We want our children engaged in exciting activities, and we want their emotional needs to be met. The natural result will be a bond that supports, not replaces, the original parent-child relationship.

Milestones

To tell or not to tell, that is always the debate. Does baby taking his first step at the center qualify as *the* first step if parents are not witness to it? If that information is not shared, do parents view the center as attempting to have the upper hand in knowing their child? Do parents feel the center is not being forthright in their exchanges? If this milestone is shared, do parents then feel left out? Do they agonize over their decision be a working parent and miss seeing all these *firsts?* The answer is "Yes" to all of the above.

Each center may have its own practice for reporting, or not, those milestones. Some will send a special certificate home stating, "I cut my first tooth today," or "I took my first step!" Others will make a phone call to parents to share the news. Some will encourage parents to uncover this revelation themselves upon arrival at the end of the day: "Maybe Helena is ready to take a step to Mommy?" Many centers believe that it truly only happens *first* when it happens for the parents, and will wait for parents to discover the breakthrough at home.

I don't believe milestone reporting should be a center practice or philosophy. It's wise when the center asks parents what their preferences are for reporting events that will naturally occur. Some will prefer not to be told—they do not want to deal with that emotional weight and would prefer to uncover it themselves. I have found that most parents do want the information shared with them. It is disconcerting to feel that others are privy to knowledge about your child to which you are not. If your center does not look for your input to these decisions, let them know how you feel, and how you want these situations handled. There is no right way, only personal preference.

Sharing Sensitive Information

The trusting relationship you have now developed with the center provides for a comfort that allows you to utilize the center's expertise. It's a safe assumption that centers and caregivers that have been providing quality care for many years to many families, including their own, have learned a thing or two! As a resource, these people can help you work through difficult times and provide much-needed insights.

Though no one expects you to bare your soul or expose private aspects and details of your life, there will be occasions when some of your child's behaviors will be a direct result of just that. Decide with whom you wish to share this information in the center, and how much of it they actually need. Sometimes just knowing there are transitions or tensions at home will be enough.

One of our toddlers had daily conversations on the play telephone with his estranged father:

"Do you hear me Richard? I said you better come and pick Jefferson up this weekend. You better play with him too! Do you hear me? Are you listening to me?"

The staff tried to role-play with Jefferson, using open-ended questions and statements to try and allow for his expression and frustrations.

Sadly, Jefferson would just shut down and withdraw into his own world. We thought if we had a better understanding of this father-son relationship, we could offer better support and help him out of his retreat.

When we shared his play with his mom, she was not only embarrassed by his mimicry of her, but also that this very personal issue was being aired in the middle of the center.

Children will bring their home life to the center. Preverbal children may act out personal disturbances through anger, aggressiveness, and withdrawal. But you can almost always count on verbal children to reveal the internal mechanics of their home life in detail. In other words, there are few safe secrets! From what was served for dinner the night before to the argument between Mom and Dad, young children love to volunteer their experiences and share them with peers and teachers, regardless of their validity. One of our preschool children declared to the class: "We're moving to a new house. It has a big porch out front, and it's far away."

When the teacher asked the parent about the impending move, she was amused to discover a museum house tour the day before had led to the inaccurate announcement.

> When the relationship between home and center is a trusting and productive one, you are safe in the knowledge that your confidentiality will be respected, and the information shared will be used only in the best interests of your child.

Making decisions about what needs to be communicated is a very personal one. For every family, that answer will be different. When the relationship between home and center is a trusting and productive one, you are safe in the knowledge that your confidentiality will be respected, and the information shared will be used only in the best interests of your child.

Baby-Sitting and the Center's Staff

The solicitation of child care staff to baby-sit in parents' homes is rarely condoned by most centers' administrative offices. It is, however, unrealistic for centers to think they are able to prevent or monitor it.

The Parents' View

Where else can you find people whom you know and trust and whom your child knows and trusts? Who else do you make contact with on a regular basis? Naturally, your child care center's staff fills those requirements. You make the obvious assumption that proper reference and background checks have been done on these people, ensuring their integrity. Approaching them during drop-off or pick-up time is fairly easy, but if you need to call them during the day, you are comfortable with making that move. They are not working (that you know of) on weekends and evenings, the perfect time for your baby-sitting needs. Then there's the possibility of getting a little inside information about the center. You know, is the rumor true that one of the coworkers is leaving soon? Can you imagine your child's delight when she sees her favorite caregiver come to her home to baby-sit! This sounds just too good to be true. You have found the perfect source for your personal baby-sitting needs!

The Staff Person's View

You do not make much money. In fact, if you weren't sharing this apartment with your friend, you would never be able to afford to live. Baby-sitting is easy, decent pay, and it doesn't interfere with your regular work hours; well, it doesn't usually. Only when the parent asks you to take off from work to watch her sick child, but she's going to pay you double what you normally make, so why not? The only time it can get sticky is when parents ask a lot of questions or want to talk about the center, other staff members, or other families at the center. But you really want them to like you, because if they like you and trust you, maybe they'll give you more hours of baby-sitting or refer you to their neighbor for additional baby-sitting! So talking to them casually about the center may only just further endear you to them!

The Center's View

You would love to mandate that no staff member will baby-sit in the homes of the families at your center. Ever. The last thing you want are your employees becoming buddy-buddy with the parents. That will undermine all the professionalism you try to maintain in the center. Before you know it, the parents will be campaigning on behalf of the staff's individual needs, and the staff will be gossiping about whose home is a pigsty. But you know that it will go underground if you do make it prohibitive, so it's probably better to make a few clearly defined rules. The most important thing you want to emphasize is the confidentiality of the staff person. Ensure that they are not divulging information (sensitive or not) about other families, staff, or practices at the center. That becomes pure rumor or hearsay and is most unprofessional. You also want to make sure that staff do not baby-sit for families during regular operating hours of the center. That's an obvious conflict of interest. The hardest part, though, is the unknown. You do trust this staff person to care for the children beautifully in a supervised environment. You have no knowledge, however, of this caregiver's personal life, and how she would be without the support, guidance, and checks and balances of the other staff members and the center itself.

The Final Decision

So now what?

I have seen very successful results of parents and staff who have entered this partnership, as well as some real bombshells. Though these teachers and caregivers are the most natural solutions to your baby-sitting dilemma and can be beneficial for both individuals, be prepared for some of the aftermath that might follow. When staff are invited into your homes for purposes other than an authorized teacher's visitation, it can compromise your relationship with the center. Have you learned something about that staff person's intent at the center that the director has not? Can you complain or put in your vote about something that you found out about *off the record?* How about using this new bias toward the staff member to influence the administrator's decision making? Some children might be favored in this group care environment because of the personal relationship now established. If that is an outcome, it is certainly unfair to the other children, who all need to be heard, seen, and appreciated equally.

Something else to consider: though you are relying on the center's reputation for having good personnel, their observations of a staff member with children is limited to group situations. They may not know how that staff member would be in a more intimate setting.

Many centers support a policy that no staff member may be alone in a room—out of earshot or vision range—with a child at any time. That's just common sense and security—security for the child, the staff person, and the center. Background checks of staff are strong indicators, but they speak to the person's known history. There are no crystal balls, and there is no reason to put children, staff, or the center in potentially damaging situations. A policy such as this eliminates any opportunities for unprofessional conduct or misinterpretations.

Guidelines

This relationship was obviously destined to be. By paying attention to a few details, you can avoid some of the glaring pitfalls:

- As with any baby-sitter, I would ask the staff person for references of people whose homes they have baby-sat in. Do your own background checks. Some good questions to ask are:

  - How did this staff member relate to the children in the home?

  - How did she relate to the adults?

  - How often did she sit for you? Over what time period?

  - Was there ever any reason to doubt this staff person's sincerity?

  - Was she reliable? Honest?

  - Were there any accidents in the home while she was in charge?

  - What was the best experience you had with her? The worst?

  - What three adjectives would you use to describe her?

- Do the answers to these questions correspond with the person you know this staff person to be?

- Do not compromise the security of this staff person's job by asking them awkward questions relating to the center, regardless of any incidents that may be occurring there.

- Keep the relationship strictly professional. Don't invite your new baby-sitter to the theater with you or to a family barbecue.

- Be honest and fair in your employment ethics. Pay the sitter as you said you would, pick them up and return home at the times you agreed to. Don't take advantage of their desire to please you by asking too much of them. ("After you feed and bathe the kids, would you mind washing the kitchen floor?") Though this may appear to be an obvious point, on the rare occasions when parents have not treated staff fairly, they are quick to share that information with their coworkers the next day.

- Lastly, don't put this staff member in an obligatory role. Very often, parents will invite a staff member to their child's birthday party outside the center. Naturally, several if not all the children from that child's class are invited to the party as well. This not only becomes another day of work for the staff person, who has to make nice-nice to all the parents and attend to all the children looking for their attention, but they are also then obligated to purchase a gift for your child. Then the other children from the class are looking for birthday presents from that staff person when it's their birthday time, even if the staff member does not attend their party. Trust me, the staff member will not be insulted if she doesn't get an invitation!

When Something Is Wrong

I would expect in many circumstances, and especially in times of uncertainty, you may question your original choice to have placed your child in this center. The normal range of insecurities will find most parents feeling this way at some time. It is the nagging doubt that refuses to let go that signals to you it may be more than just a passing insecurity. Maybe everything seemed fine at first, or maybe your hopes for the situation were "Things will get better," but they didn't. I think many parents second-guess their decision making when forming such a monumental one! Painful separation each morning, center phones not being answered promptly (having to talk to voice mail!), and the center opening five minutes late (on the morning you have an important early appointment) can be most annoying. Clothing getting lost or confused with other children's, or a teacher you may not have yet warmed up to (even though your child may have) is unsettling at best. Such irritations, however, are usually short-lived, and can be worked out with the administration and caregivers through good communication.

We know children rely on stability and continuity from their caregivers to achieve success in child care. There will be times, though, that this continuity must be sacrificed for care that you believe in. How can you know when a change is necessary and appropriate? Depending on the situation, you may not know for sure, but some guidelines and your gut instinct will assist your decision.

> We know children rely on stability and continuity from their caregivers to achieve success in child care. There will be times, though, that this continuity must be sacrificed for care that you believe in.

Safety

Your child is getting injured too often. I am not talking about the occasional scratch or scrape of the knee. Children will be children. One-year-olds learning to walk seem to tumble at every corner, two-year-olds acquiring their language skills have difficulty in expressing themselves and will resort to aggressive and emotional outbursts, and we know about the four-year-old's tendency toward bold and defiant behavior. It is difficult to protect our children from the usual bumps and bruises at home, where there is only one of them and one of us! Certainly in a group situation, there are more children with fewer adults, so isn't there more opportunity for those bumps and scrapes to occur? Well, yes and no. Statistics have shown us that children at home with a parent will get more injuries than a child in a child care center. Remember in chapter 1, "The Decision"? The dual roles at home (household chores and child care) are distracting, while providers in a center setting have a single role of child care. The contact

One mom, Mrs. G., came to our center with an incredible example of a center where there was clearly too much injury.

"Over a period of several weeks, each day, my daughter Sondra would come home with yet another wound. The daily range of injuries would vary between several bites to a gash in her head. There was no written explanation to accompany these bruises, nor did any staff member at the site have knowledge as to their origin. They blamed these occurrences on my two-year-old daughter's feistiness, and told me they can't be expected to see everything that goes on. Unsure of my own knowledge in child development, and attributing some difficulty to my language barrier, I remained in the center. Until yesterday. Sondra's dad picked her up from child care as he normally would. He noticed she seemed to be talking funny on the car ride home, but seemed OK other than that. When they arrived home, I went to look inside Sondra's mouth to see why she was speaking so awkwardly. When I realized her tongue had been punctured, either by her own teeth or an object, I immediately called the center. One staff member told me she knew Sondra had fallen, but the assistant director took care of her, and she did not know the specifics. I was unable to contact the assistant director until the next morning. Upon contact, the assistant director professed to have no knowledge of this fall or of the injury."

It was obvious that this child was in a center where there was a lack of adequate supervision. On top of the apparent insufficient and negligent care, the administration's responsibility in not following through and communicating these injuries to Sondra's parents was inexcusable.

Time for a change.

with other children, though, in the center may provide for different types of injuries, such as biting, nail scratching, or pushing. In a center where the ratios are good and the caregivers are attentive to the children, these instances should be under control, with staff and parents working together when a problem is developing. In other words, there should not be a daily *Ouch* report for your child.

Personnel

It could be your critical nature, but lately you don't believe so. You have witnessed staff yelling at children, accompanied by finger shaking in the face. Their tone of voice depicts anger, not firmness, and the children and staff do not appear to get much pleasure from each other's company.

The other extreme in the staff's performance that concerns you isn't as intimidating but is just as upsetting. Several apathetic, uninvolved caregivers stare out into space, oblivious of the children in their care. You believe one may have even fallen asleep while in this mode. The children randomly wander the class and the playground, searching for something to involve them. A relationship does not seem to have developed, let alone a bond with these caregivers.

Then there is the change in your child's behavior and disposition at home. Since he started this center he has become clingy and weepy. He is not even in that nine- to nineteen-month age group where separation and stranger anxieties are heightened and these behaviors are more expected. Nor does it appear to be a manipulating tactic to stay home with Mom.

When you bring your concerns to the attention of the director, she offers a defensive explanation for the behavior, dismisses it as unworthy of her time, or promises to look into it, but never does.

Time for a change.

Philosophy

Maybe the staff are nice enough, and perhaps your child is doing well. Making a change under these circumstances is much more difficult to justify. There are some practices in this center, however, that you cannot seem to get past. Like disregarding your instructions. Why is staff still feeding your baby his bottle while he is in the infant seat? You were very specific that you wanted him in the caregiver's arms for bottle feeding at all times. Then they promised you that your baby would not go in the infant swing, and you walked in at the end of one day to find him sitting in it. That daily dosage of television viewing is really bothering you. Originally, the director told you the children watch just an occasional short interactive video, but that's not the case. Why are you paying so much money to a center for loving, interactive, and educational care, just to have them park the children in front of a passive entertainment box? What happened to the learning through play philosophy they had professed to subscribe to? Why are these children required to sit at the tables for what appears to be infinite amounts of time? Maybe you could have tolerated some of this, but when your three-year-old came home with homework and instructions to practice his letters with a parent because he was not doing as well as the others, you knew.

Time for a change.

Centers like the ones mentioned illustrate extreme versions (and hopefully rare ones) of **Red Light Warnings!** These institutions masquerading as child care centers are easy to identify when you possess knowledge and understanding of what to look for and expect (as you now do!).

Logistics

Depending on your work schedule, you may find it beneficial to find a center near your home or near your workplace. You need to find one that is open the hours you need, is affordable, and subscribes to your general philosophy. How great! You are one of the fortunate ones who has made a wonderful

Eighteen-month-old Jacob had been coming to our center since he was eight weeks old. His family lived an hour away, but Mom worked close by. This was a wonderful arrangement for Jacob's mom. Every evening she would pick him up about ten minutes before closing. Jacob was naturally tired from his long day at the center, and with the lull of the car ride, he enjoyed a peaceful slumber all the way home. Mom benefited from that silent hour by shifting gears and reflecting quietly on her day. Upon arriving home, Jacob was refreshed, energized, and full of playfulness for Mom and Dad. Their time together was enjoyed by each of them.

As Jacob approached eighteen months, he no longer seemed to need this nap. The ride home became more and more challenging as Mom tried to distract and entertain him. Then came the occasional traffic jam, where they would sit in the car for up to two and a half hours. Jacob's mood, to say the least, deteriorated. After a two-hour crying bout all the way home one evening, it became apparent that this family needed to make a change.

match with a center. Your child is doing well, and you couldn't be happier, until one day.

When your child is thriving and contented in an environment, it makes making necessary changes more painful. The reality of life, though, is that people will experience many modifications to their jobs, homes, and income levels. When these factors affect your ability to provide consistent child care for your child, treat the adjustment as you would any transition. Talk to your child about the imminent change and gradually introduce him to the new setting. Children will fare well under difficult circumstances outside the home if their family is consistent and intact, supportive, and sensitive to the needs of each other.

9

The Success

Children Thriving
in Child Care Centers

From the parent of a one-year-old in child care:

"We were at a party, and there were at least five or six kids the same age—none of the children were in child care except for mine. There was no question of how much more adjusted Corey was than the other children. They were afraid of their shadows! Not one would venture away from Mom for a second. They cried any time someone other than their parent came near them! There Corey was, making friends and playing. He was so comfortable and happy. I know it's because of child care; he's exposed to loving people other than his family every day."

I have heard this story from many parents over the years. I do believe there is more to a well-adjusted one-year-old, though than just having a good child care center on his résumé. As parents, we can be competitive about our children, even looking for flaws in other children to boost ours. We often look for reasons to justify the guilt that never seems to stop plaguing us. However, children in child care centers will tend to acquire some skills earlier than their non-center peers.

Eventually everyone catches up, and it's each child's own individuality that stands out.

Parents who have had the experience of a center that meets their needs, reflects high quality, and is truly nurturing know how children can and do bloom in such a setting. For each child, that blossom will be unique. The fact is, children do thrive in warm and caring group environments outside the home. When we get past the need to be responsible and in control of each of their successes, we can better appreciate those achievements.

> The fact is, children do thrive in warm and caring group environments outside the home.

Most parents in centers do feel their children have profited from being in such a setting. Parents new to child care, though, are in a difficult situation, with many emotional issues to deal with. Many times guilt and anxiety cloud parents' vision of their children responding so positively to the center life. It is beneficial to hear from *seasoned* parents in these instances.

The Toddler's Success

Independence Issues

This issue is better known as "I can do it myself!" What parent of a two- to three-year-old child has not heard that statement before? Yet as we are charging out the door in the morning, we may have run out of time (and patience) to let our persevering toddler figure out which way the shirt goes on. We then need to be the parent, put the shirt on him (probably as he is ranting and raving at us), scurry to get to child care and still make the train. These common battles are not always ideally handled.

Asserting the need for autonomy is a natural part of children's separation process. Yet circumstances don't always permit them to realize that need. Succeeding at tasks that may appear small to an adult are often monumental to a child. We are reminded of this when we witness their expression, after they have mastered something like putting their

One of our dads had the good fortune of being home with his son the first year. They were a team! They ran errands together, played, and enjoyed their time in each other's company. The unavoidable came, Dad had to resume his career, and baby was transitioned into our center. It was one of the more difficult transitions, and took about a month until baby and Dad were really comfortable. Several months later, Dad approached me with his "confession."

"I didn't think anyone other than myself could take care of my son. He was such a happy little boy. I feared going back to work, and that by enrolling him in a program, I would be sacrificing some of that happiness. I didn't sacrifice it! The center just gave him more reasons to stay that way."

coat on for the first time. It shouts *triumph!* Children love making choices and being in charge of their destination. The toddler who is pondering his choices between playing in the block corner or housekeeping area is no longer without a say! When controlled choices are offered, the need for a power struggle is often eliminated. Some choices could be:

- Do you want peanut butter or tuna for lunch?

- Would you like to wear the red smock or the blue one?

- Which of these blankets would you like for nap time?

Just the nature of a child care center offers great possibilities for children's independence. Opportunities to help themselves in a variety of situations are more readily available. Because there is not one-on-one care, needs are not anticipated as quickly as they are when at home with Mom. Taking their jackets on and off, hanging their coat in their cubby, pouring their own juice, and cleaning their place after lunch are just some of the self-help skills that provide independence and foster a positive self-esteem. Parents can facilitate this for their children by giving them safe choices to make at home and providing opportunities for successful completion of simple chores.

A parent of one of our very articulate toddlers shared a story with me. This mom was very conscientious about following through at home with words and phrases that we used at the center. She loved giving her daughter responsibilities and *safe choices* to make at home. One day while Mom was climbing on the kitchen counter trying to change a recessed light bulb, her daughter came in, looked up at her, then shook her head in disappointment and said, "Mom, I don't think you are making a very safe choice!"

As comical as we both knew this reaction from her daughter was, it also reminded us that this toddler was thinking. She was processing and determining the safety of the situation. Her evaluation was clearly "This is not safe."

By expecting children to be responsible for the choices we offer them, we are asking them to first take stock and assess their surrounding circumstances. Then they need to determine which choice is best for them. A fairly complex process for a young child, but it feels great to be empowered!

> Asserting the need for autonomy is a natural part of children's separation process.

Dependence Issues

At times, a parent may fight her child's independence: by deciding for the child what clothes they should wear each day; providing difficult clothing that makes dressing themselves not possible; or offering them meals that require an adult to feed them. Independence may be viewed to some as a negative rather than a positive outcome of child care centers. After all, once our children begin doing more and more for themselves, they will need us less. The need to feel indispensable to our child sometimes compensates for the guilt we carry by leaving them.

One mom of a two-year-old hesitated with each advancement her daughter made. She was sad when she was told her daughter put on her own coat. She felt she was too young to be asked to do such a thing.

We were pushing her child to grow up. Though we called and shared her daughter's jubilation and pride when she exclaimed, "Look at me! Look at what I did!", Mom couldn't witness this because she did not allow her daughter the opportunity to do the same in her presence. She was convinced her daughter must be performing this task under duress. It was important that this mom understood we were not *requiring* her daughter to put on her own jacket. It was part of the natural progression of independence and self-help skills that children gravitate toward. They will see other children doing something, and they naturally want to do it too. Besides, it feels good to do something by yourself! We asked Mom to observe her daughter from the viewing window one day. Her daughter could not see her. The group was finishing a song in circle time when the teacher said, "We are going to get our coats on now." She witnessed as her daughter joyfully jumped up from the circle and grabbed her coat. Tears came to her eyes as she watched her daughter throw it on the floor upside down, push her arms through the sleeves, and sing, "I'm ready!" She saw how proud her daughter was of herself. She *was* ready. Mom had not been.

Children will naturally volley back and forth from independence to dependence. One moment they will yearn to do something on their own, another they may curl up and refuse to even entertain the thought. They want to do things for themselves, but they must have their caregiver nearby, providing reassurance. We must provide them with appropriate choices to make and simple tasks to conquer. Calmly we need to support them when they need to rely on us, offer them the words they need, and give empathy toward their feelings. When attempts at tasks appear hopeless, we must applaud their efforts. The end result of children acquiring more independence is an acquisition of new skills, readiness to try new things without fear of failing, and a positive self-esteem.

Self-Help Skills

Similar to the little girl who took such delight in putting on her own jacket is a child's pride at being able to open one's own lunch box, pull apart the foil wrapping on a sandwich, peel away the top of a yogurt, clean up in the bathroom, put away toys, or get dressed. These are all skills that help the child help themselves. What a great feeling it is too.

Children are used to, and expect, Mom or Dad to do for them. After all, *that is their job!* But when caregivers are present, the expectations are not as passionate. For a child to learn about his own abilities, caregivers must resist doing everything for him. This can give a child license to attempt to do something they otherwise might not have had the courage to. Children in child care centers will accomplish these skills with greater ease. Not because they are required to, but because there is greater opportunity to do so.

At the lunch tables, twelve toddlers and three staff are seated. Obviously three adults cannot assist twelve children at the same time. There is time for each child to make attempts at opening their lunch, pouring their milk, and then wiping up the spill! At snack time, one child may pass out napkins, another cups. Several small containers of juice are available for children to serve themselves. A responsive caregiver will guide the children to accomplishing these tasks successfully, until they are able to and chose to do it independently.

> Whenever possible, toddlers and preschool children should be encouraged to work out their difficulties themselves.

Problem Solving

When clear limits are set and realistic expectations of behavior are defined, circumstances are in place for children to make decisions and solve their own problems. Whenever possible, toddlers and preschool children should be encouraged to work out their difficulties themselves. This is the first step in a lifetime of problem solving. Even the youngest of toddlers are assisted with words:

TEACHER:	You are angry that Matt took the book from you.
TODDLER:	Nods head
TEACHER:	Can you use your words to tell Matt how you feel?
TODDLER:	I want the book!

The teacher is giving words to the toddler's feelings and validating those feelings. This toddler is learning two important things. First, someone understands his frustration. Then, he realizes that he possesses the ability to resolve the issue himself.

Walking to the block area, a three-year-old pushes another child. The other child gets obviously angry and expresses his feelings.

TEACHER: Why did you push Brian?

CHILD: I don't want him to knock over the block building I made.

TEACHER: Can you think what else you could have done, other than pushing him to let him know that?

CHILD, THINKS A MOMENT: I could have asked him to walk around it.

Teachers can assist children in searching for positive solutions to everyday obstacles. This teacher is offering the child who pushed the opportunity to come up with an alternate method for his original problem solving. A group care environment puts children in positions of needing these skills earlier. However, when acquired, these skills cross over to other areas in the child's life in which they may experience challenges.

Enrichment

As much as we might like to believe we could offer a similar balance of enriching activities and opportunities for our own children at home, chances are, we probably cannot. After all, when we are home with our children, we have many things to take care of, and they won't all revolve around our child. This is expected.

One of our moms walked into the toddler room earlier than usual to pick up her child one afternoon. Five children, including hers, were gathered around a large table with a staff member. They were squishing their hands through globs of green finger paint mixed with shaving cream. There was obvious delight in each of the young children's actions, as they giggled at every glob that fell to the floor or flew on their nose. As the mother stood back to enjoy the moment, she whispered to me: "This is why my daughter comes to you. No way could I let her do this in my house!"

It is the sole responsibility of the caregivers and teachers to take care of the children. They plan the entire day around them! This is their job. With loving hands, caregivers are nurturing, reading, and playing with babies while they investigate their environment. Qualified teachers have programmed meaningful exploration, fun music and song, and group projects that take on real significance in the child's young life. This kind of age-appropriate exposure allows for a variety of learning experiences for the child in a center-based program.

Social Skills and Friendships

One of the greatest gifts a group care environment can give to children is the ability to be comfortable with other children and adults. Like the mom at the beginning of this chapter who noticed social differences between her child care child and the other children, this skill will tend to come easier and sooner to these children.

With toddlers, socializing with peers is not a natural phenomenon. They are still very self-centered, and do not understand the concept of sharing until almost three years old. Grabbing a toy from another child (especially if it is theirs) is instinctive to this age group. They may not even like or want that toy until the child sitting next to them expresses an interest in it! Arguments are bound to start. In center-based programs, several toys of the same kind should be available to children. This minimizes the tug-of-war conflicts and reduces the need for them to *wait their turn*. When two or more children have the same toy, it then becomes conducive to interactive play. A responsive caregiver should be close by to assist in redirecting the children if and when necessary. She should encourage cooperation and help them interact in a playful manner: by joining in the fun as one of the players adds even more to the enjoyment.

Valuable relationships begin to form when children spend time together as a group, and in one-on-one interaction. As they see other children on a regular basis, relationships progress. Friendship takes place. At the most innocent level of childhood, these children are learning to rely on one another, care about each other, problem-solve together, and most importantly, enjoy each other's company!

Our center takes babies six weeks old up to kindergarten-age children at six years old. Many of our children have grown from infancy to kindergarten together. When the time approaches for these children to *leave the nest* and move on to their respective first grades, there is a sadness along with the joy. Parents and teachers realize the special kinship these children have formed and know the reality and likelihood of their long-term continuance is not assured.

The relationship that develops between caregivers and children is the initiation of the child's connection with adults outside the family. When these adults are consistent, and support the varying levels of play that children journey through, it becomes a positive connection. There are typically several adults to which the child care center child will have exposure. Socializing with grown-ups becomes very natural and nonthreatening.

Trust

Imagine how much less complicated life would be if we all could predict the world around us. We would know each of the people we encounter, how those people will react to us, and what limitations exist. Of course that is not possible or desirable. It is ideal, though, for a young baby. When children can anticipate that their needs will be acknowledged and responded to, trust will follow. In warm, responsive environments, caregivers and teachers have the opportunity to establish relationships with each individual child. They know each child's requirements and are prepared to react to them in a positive, loving manner. Consistency of care in a center is paramount to making that happen, but it is also the most challenging aspect of a child care center.

Acceptance of Diversity

My son had been in the center with the same children since he was a baby. His friends in the program came from very diverse backgrounds and cultures. These kids learned how to drink from a cup at the same time, proceeded through the potty years as a team, explored the worms and dirt together as they researched our playground, and developed their individual personalities side by side. One evening on the ride home, Michael, now four and a half, asked me about one of these little girls, "Mom, how come Natalie has brown on her skin?"

"What do you mean Mike?"

"How come she has brown on her skin and I don't?"

There was no judgment in his question; it was just an observation he made.

Though we had shared and celebrated the cultural differences of many of our families, he had never before realized that they truly were *differences,* and he couldn't understand the reason for it. He was just first noticing the physical distinction between himself and his friend.

Centers should strive naturally to represent many cultures in the program. The use of stories, music, food, and art that depict diversity are beginning steps for children learning to respect backgrounds other than their own. Children respond with great fascination and excitement when a parent comes to the center and shares a family tradition with them. The population of a center alone may make it culturally diverse. In communities where there is less diversity, greater efforts to infuse diversity should be made through programming, thereby bringing awareness and sensitivity to our children.

Caregivers need to be sensitive to respecting cultural differences among the center's families as well. This is demonstrated when each family is valued and celebrated without judgment.

When a setting positively represents diversity, then acceptance and tolerance will develop. Children cannot comprehend the grown-up world and the values that adults might place on peoples differences. Because center-based kids are typically exposed to diversity at an early age, their understanding for respect and tolerance toward others is, we hope, an unbiased one.

The Young Baby's Success

Socialization

Yes, even babies socialize! Because he is totally dependent on the adults in his life for all his needs, baby's entire world revolves around these adults.

Who better to rock and roll with? The relationship that babies develop with just one or few caregivers is a social and loving one. These people get to know the baby as an individual. It is with this knowledge that they are able to respond appropriately to him. They play social games like peek-a-boo. Feeding and changing are highlights as caregivers converse with baby. The simple routines like these offer unique opportunities to have one-on-one care in a group setting. Good caregivers take advantage of this time and make it pleasurable for themselves and baby. Smiles and gurgles are responded to similarly. Reading a story, singing a lullaby, or looking at a shiny toy together becomes a joyful interaction between the two, and very endearing. When baby's need is for quiet looking-in-the-mirror time, that special adult recognizes baby's need for down time, and is able to stand back and watch.

Yes, even babies socialize!

On the floor, each holding their own toy, or sitting side by side in the high chairs during meal time babies are learning about socialization with other babies. They may not look at each other or notice each other. In pursuit of a toy, they will probably climb over each other as if the other one wasn't even there! Yet they are learning about each other and their environment at the same time. From the very onset, babies are most social little people.

Trust

Many centers are moving toward keeping young children with the same caregivers for longer periods of time, at least for the first two years. We have learned much over the years about continuity of care and the value it has in providing stability for young children. We have also learned how important those first few years are to a developing baby. When there is little staff turnover in a center, children gain consistency. They can then forecast how, when, and by whom their needs will be met. Expectations are developed based on how the caregivers in their life treat them. Anticipation of warm, nurturing care lets baby know he is taken care of. Frequent and responsive interaction makes baby feel she can have an effect on her environment. A caregiver's response to baby's personality is creating trust in the environment as well as in the adults. When parents have found a center and caregivers with these characteristics, babies cannot help but thrive. Their success is obvious when we witness caregiver and baby sharing joy and comfort in each other's company.

The Parents' Success

Start Networking!

I received a call from a parent one day; he was very enthusiastic. He just read our monthly newsletter and was interested in a proposal that was written by another one of our parents. The proposal was for the initiation of a parent network that would represent the parents as a group. Their purpose would be to work with the administration toward specific goals like fund-raising, volunteer work days, parent education, staff appreciation, and more. Parents would benefit from a swap page in each newsletter. This would help them to recycle baby clothing, furniture, and other items among themselves, organize social gatherings for the center's families, create and promote special events, and be a general support for new parents.

This parent thought it was great and wanted to sign up! It took me a second to gather my thoughts, but then I realized and shared with him that the newsletter he was referring to was four months old. There had been no response to the original proposal four months ago, and so nothing was done about it.

You are in good company if the burdens of work and home do not keep you on top of the reading pile in the kitchen. Parents express the desire to be involved in their child's program, but often have a difficult time jump-starting an effort. With the best of intentions, many will volunteer for duties they simply are unable to follow through on. It is not necessarily reflective of an apathetic parent body, but rather the result of working many hours and being a parent to a young child.

It took us about a year to get a parent network off the ground. Once in the air, though, it soared! Parents began to realize how they were each other's best resources. This committee was organized by just two parents who took it upon themselves to add a Parent Network page to our monthly newsletter. They established once-a-month social gatherings at nearby areas of interest with their children. As their children became socialized, so did their parents. Many of our families were new to the area and were in need of adult companionship outside the office. Their children already knew each other. Now they had an opportunity to become acquainted as well. Pot-luck dinners were organized, picnics, spring fests, and more. A Parents' Night Out baby-sitting co-op was established, in which parents took turns watching each other's children for an evening so they could each get a night out without the children. (The kids loved this one too!) A Parent Network bulletin board was prominently featured in our lobby for last-minute news and events.

> If there is not an active parent body in place, you can start one!

Parents enlisted parents as fund-raising efforts brought in large donations for the center. They chose to draft each other in a major attempt to increase parent participation. Though not all parents were flexible or available, everyone did what they could. Some of our part-time working parents volunteered to help out in their child's classroom on their days off. Other parents volunteered to make flyers at their office for upcoming events, plant a garden in our playground, initiate a staff-recognition program, and even research parent education topics.

When you become a part of a center, you will probably have choices as to the amount and kind of participation you will need to contribute. Socializing, networking, and having other parents available as a sounding board may not be ideal for all. Many parents work extremely long hours, have trouble keeping up with their existing friends and family, and are not looking to add more responsibilities to their already rare free time.

For most parents, however, it is refreshing to participate in relationships with people who live in their communities and whose children attend the same center. Having social events, baby-sitting co-ops, used furniture swaps, and parent-to-parent advice close by can be instrumental in solidifying a parent body.

You may have the opportunity to be involved at some level in your child's program. Each program will have its own philosophy and guidelines for parental input and participation. Some centers will have a parent group that plays a part in the staff interviewing process. Some parent groups have voting rights as policies are made and changed. Other centers have a parent service committee that arranges for opportunities for families to:

- Drop off and pick up dry cleaning at the center

- Have take-out dinner delivered to the site for parents to pick up upon arriving to the center in the evening

- Obtain haircuts for kids at the site during center hours.

If there is not an active parent body in place, you can start one! Talk to the director and share your thoughts and goals. Ask to survey the parents to determine what their needs are, and how much participation you could expect. This is a great step toward strengthening communication between parents and the center. The more parental input there is, the more likely parents' voices will be heard, respected, and responded to, and the more likely that the program will reflect the needs of the families it serves.

10

The Home Stretch

School-Age Child Care

He may be bigger and older, but your six-year-old is hardly in a position to care for himself after school. Each child reaches different levels of maturity at different times in his or her life. You realize the need to provide adult guidance for those afternoon or early-morning hours when you are at work.

Your search for and evaluation of appropriate before- and after-school care is quite different than it was several years ago when you were looking for infant care. Both yours and your child's needs for care have changed too. You are no longer concerned with sterile surfaces, potty-training theories, and safety latches on cabinets. Your judgment of caregivers is not based on locating the most loving and nurturing individual and environment, but rather on engaging the most safety-conscious and experienced teacher who will provide wonderful opportunities for your child after school.

What also concerns you is:

• Keeping your child in a safe and well-supervised environment

• Wanting an enriching and fun recreational experience for him

- Seeing her engaged in creative new interests

- Finding a place where he has opportunity to get some home-work done, with a little help if needed

- Ensuring she has opportunities to play outside and get her *yah yahs* out

- Promoting his happiness

The options for before- and after-school care can be much different than for preschool-aged children and babies. There are many private child care centers providing school-age child care (SACC) programs, as well as some family pro-viders who will care for a larger range in ages of children. PTAs have been attempting to add this to their school's list of services, some successfully, others not. You will find that community recre-ation departments, YMCAs, and many churches and synagogues provide SACC as well. Those that offer organized and well-supervised programs with curriculum and trained staff rate much higher than those that are merely cafeterias with fifty chil-dren running around, who are then forced to sit and do homework the rest of their time.

> The options for before- and after-school care can be much different than for preschool-aged children and babies.

YMCAs are presently the largest private organization providing school-aged child care in this country. Many will operate on-site of the public school your child is in, or have the children bused to their site. JCCs and Boys and Girls Clubs operate similarly. It makes sense to gravitate to those operations that are run by organizations that are heavily committed to this cause. Their past experience and current in-vestment weighs heavily when determining the kind of experience your child will have.

Look for the programs that offer choices and flexibility in the chil-dren's afternoons. When children are sitting in a classroom all day doing work, they need a place to retreat to afterward where they are comfortable and have more say in the structure. Some of these pro-grams may offer enrichment opportunities for the children. These

Look for the programs that offer choices and flexibility in the children's afternoons.

could consist of art classes, karate, basketball, jewelry making, rocketry, and more! There are many new and innovative school-aged curriculums being promoted through several initiatives to improve quality in SACC programs.

Lastly, talk to the families in your community. Find out what the working parents of school-aged children are doing to help with this issue. Get references for the programs in your neighborhood, and see where your child's friends are going to be.

11

Making It Work

Some Final Thoughts

Taking the plunge when making that final decision to return to work, whether you are leaving your first newborn baby or your third child of preschool age, is not easy. It's a decision that has you up at nights worrying and anticipating, and imagining scenarios that you would rather not.

- What if . . . my child gets sick, gets hurt, needs me, is looking for me, is angry at me for leaving her?

- What if . . . I can't get to her quick enough?

- What if . . . I don't go back to work, is it even possible?

- What if . . . something happens to me??

- Who will pay the bills, could we get along with less?

- What about my career? . . . Am I ready to retire, even temporarily, after all that time and hard work?

These thoughts and others can haunt you until you have reconciled with your ultimate decision. And not to worry, everybody will have an opinion too. You will need to weigh and filter all of the information that well-intentioned friends, acquaintances, and family bestow upon you. You and your partner will formulate your own opinions and your own goals for your family.

As you progress and embark upon your child care center search and evaluation for the perfect match, you will be amazed at how much you have learned just by taking the time to do it right! You will instinctively feel the warmth of the center that values its families. When families are viewed by the child care center as pivotal to the child's life and the success of the center, a strong partnership can go forward with the mutual goals of supporting the child, the family, child care, and the workplace. The center that meets all of your requirements and fits your style will be worth all of the time and energy you invested. It will most likely be the more exceptional one that not only fits *all* of your needs but conforms to each of the ideals mentioned in previous chapters. So—some sacrifices are then made (preferably not too many!) and your priorities may need additional reevaluation.

Here are some extra tips for making child care center life work:

- Take time to get to know your child's teachers, and have them get to know you. You would never tell your neighbor, "I am leaving my child with somebody, but I'm not quite sure who, and the person I am leaving them with doesn't know anything about me or our family!"

- Maintain communication with your child's caregivers and teachers. Changes in home life will certainly affect a child's behavior at the center. Give the staff the right tools and information to help your child during those transitional times.

- Don't try and make up a *lost day* with your child during those few hours in the evening. Brett's mom called me one morning. She was upset that when she and her two-year-old daughter got home each evening, her daughter was *off the wall.* She explained, "I try talking to her about her day, read stories, play some of her favorite musical tapes, watch a fun movie, and just try and play with her. She will have none of it, and is mostly just whiny and crabby. I don't understand, the teachers tell me she is not like this at all during the day." Brett was telling her mom she had had enough play and stimulation for the day. She just needed to be with her mother. I suggested tossing her tapes and toys and trying to create a calmer evening for them. Shut off the television and the telephone, maybe put on some quiet classical music, keep the lighting dim, and relax together. When her mom called me the following morning to report the drastic positive change in her child's behavior, she shared, "I guess I hoped that I could squeeze in all the things I thought I should be doing with her, the things I rarely have time for. I suppose I wasn't thinking of where she was at. She was just happy to sit with me!"

The center that meets all your requirements and fits your style will be worth all of the time and energy you invested.

- Don't undermine the center with words, attitudes, or actions; they will be clearly read by your child. Work out any differences with the administration or teaching staff, and discuss with others only out of the presence of your child. Parents have the power to set their children up for failure or success depending on their approach to situations. If your toddler is aware of your difficulties or challenges at the center, how do you think she might feel when you leave her there for the day?

- Aim to bring your child and pick him up from the center the same time most days. Children who have routines and know what to expect from their day have much easier transitions.

- Become involved in the center. An uninvolved parent is usually an uninformed one. Don't risk having decisions for the center be made without you. Find a way to stay involved, informed, and active in the center to ensure your family's representation. It doesn't have to be a large amount of time that needs investing, but it might take a keen awareness.

Some parents will find the adjustment of going back to work and being part of a child care center more challenging than others. You know yourself and your child better than anybody ever could. Use that knowledge to ease into the new situation in a manner that is comfortable for both of you. Set yourself up for success! Give yourself the luxury of whatever time you have to indulge your needs.

There is a jar in the middle of the conference table in my office. It is sealed and halfway filled with potpourri. In large, bold letters, a sign is taped to the front of it that reads, "This Jar Is Half Full!" It is a reminder to all who come in my office that circumstances are often our perception of them. We can look at things any way we choose. Situations are not always going to favor us, and we need to view things in a way that will afford us the best opportunity for success. Why not seek to manage our surroundings in a positive manner?

> The greatest gift we can give to our children is independence.

Watching our children grow and evolve brings so many pleasures to parents. We are often then surprised by our own reactions to their increasing autonomy. We naturally want them to thrive and be happy, but as their attachments and success with others are not dependent on us, a bit of sadness creeps in, reminding us how quickly time goes by. The greatest gift we can give to our children is independence. Their ability to move away from dependency toward independence is a result of the security they have been given from early on. These children know it is safe to venture out. Someone was always there for them, and always will be. Our babies crawl farther away, barely looking over their shoulders, and our preschool children can't be bothered to look up from their play and wave good-bye to us. Our school-aged children begin to prefer the company of *others,* and our young adult children begin to make intelligent decisions on their own. This gravitation toward independence acquaints children with the skills they need to cope with stress.

Being working parents, we can't help but worry whether we are doing the right thing for our children and for ourselves! I think all parents share those same worries. In the course of attempting to "bring home the bacon, and fry it up in the pan," it's easy to slip off of the stove.

Following are some tips for creating balance in your life:

- Find a way to take time for yourself each week. Maybe it's a daily walk, an hour curled up reading a favorite book, or a little gardening. You will be amazed at the healing and preventative powers of some personal time.

- Make opportunities for just you and your partner or other adult. Baby-sitting co-ops through the center can help assure an evening out for you.

- Try and make a routine of dinner most nights together as a family. Even if it's just pizza! It's a wonderful habit to get into, and it is not dependent on a several-course meal or hours in the kitchen. Sitting down and making the time to share your day becomes a communal ritual that I believe contributes to keeping a family together.

- Know when to say, "No!" No, not to your child, but to your boss or coworkers. Many of us are in the habit of taking on more than our share. Now is the time to change that tendency toward overburdening ourselves with additional responsibilities.

- Solicit help. Don't be a martyr. If you don't ask for assistance, don't expect anyone to know you need it. We all have our own priorities. I have always believed that the youngest of children can help. Two- and three-year-olds folding laundry and setting the table with you not only assists in getting the tasks done, but becomes endearing time together talking and doing. If your partner is not used to carrying half the burden for chores, this is the time to change that inclination. School-age children are a wonderful assistance for preparing meals, caring for animals, cleaning up, and making beds. Not only are you getting some help, you are building responsibility in your children.

It's not easy, but things worth having rarely are. As much as I love working, and as much as I love my family, I have reconciled with the fact there is no question that we cannot have it all. Something has to give. Maybe it's not being irritated by the beds that go unmade all day. Or the take out dinners that find you craving a home-cooked meal. It could be the pile of laundry or the pile of bills mixed in with the junk mail that you are just too exhausted to sift through. For me, it's the garden of flowers and vegetables that I keep promising to plant, but never seem to get around to. Well, maybe one day.

> It's not easy, but things worth having rarely are.

As working parents, we make sacrifices, and our standards may need some adjustments to be realistic. Keep your priorities front and center at all times. You are now able to proceed to the child care center armed with additional insight and guidance. I hope you can embrace this challenging and emotional issue with comfort, understanding, and success.

12

State Licensing Standards

Child to Staff Ratio and Group Size Requirements (by State)

State	Age of Children								
	6 wks.	9 mos.	18 mos.	27 mos.	3 yrs.	4 yrs.	5 yrs.	6 yrs.	7 yrs.
Alabama	6:1	6:1	8:1	8:1	12:1	20:1	20:1	22:1	22:1
	6	6	8	8	12	20	20	22	22
Alaska	5:1	5:1	6:1	6:1	10:1	10:1	15:1	20:1	20:1
	NR	NR	NR	NR	NR	NR	NR	NR	NR
Arizona	5:1/ 11:2	6:1/ 13:2	8:1	13:1	15:1	20:1	20:1	20:1	
	NR	NR	NR	NR	NR	NR	NR	NR	NR
Arkansas	6:1	6:1	9:1	12:1	12:1	15:1	18:1	20:1	20:1
	NR	NR	NR	NR	NR	NR	NR	NR	NR
California	4:1	4:1	6:1	6:1	12:1	12:1	12:1	14:1/ 28:2	
	NR	NR	NR	NR	NR	NR	NR	NR	NR
*Colorado	5:1	5:1	5:1	7:1	10:1	12:1	15:1	15:1	15:1
	10	10	10	14	20	24	30	30	30
Connecticut	4:1	4:1	4:1	4:1	10:1	10:1	10:1	10:1	10:1
	8	8	8	8	20	20	20	20	20

Child to Staff Ratio and Group Size Requirements (by State)

State	Age of Children								
	6 wks.	9 mos.	18 mos.	27 mos.	3 yrs.	4 yrs.	5 yrs.	6 yrs.	7 yrs.
Delaware	4:1	4:1	7:1	10:1	12:1	15:1	25:1	25:1	25:1
	NR	NR	NR	NR	NR	NR	NR	NR	NR
District of	4:1	4:1	4:1	4:1	8:1	10:1	15:1	15:1	15:1
Columbia	8	8	8	8	16	20	25	30	30
Florida	4:1	4:1	6:1	11:1	15:1	20:1	25:1	25:1	25:1
	NR	NR	NR	NR	NR	NR	NR	NR	NR
Georgia	6:1	6:1	8:1	10:1	15:1	18:1	20:1	25:1	25:1
	12	12	16	20	30	36	40	50	50
*Hawaii	NA	4:1–8	6:1–12	8:1	12:1	16:1	20:1	20:1	20:1
(I/T programs separate from centers)				NR	NR	NR	NR	NR	NR
Idaho	6:1	6:1	6:1	12:1	12:1	12:1	18:1	18:1	18:1
	NR	NR	NR	NR	NR	NR	NR	NR	NR
Illinois	4:1	4:1	5:1	8:1	10:1	10:1	20:1	20:1/30:2	
	12	12	15	16	20	20	20	30	
Indiana	4:1	5:1	5:1	5:1	10:1	12:1	15:1	20:1	20:1
	8	10	10	15	NR	NR	NR	NR	NR
Iowa	4:1	4:1	4:1	6:1	8:1	12:1	15:1	15:1	15:1
	NR	NR	NR	NR	NR	NR	NR	NR	NR
Kansas	3:1	3:1	5:1	7:1	12:1	12:1	14:1	16:1	16:1
	9	9	10	14	24	24	28	32	32
Kentucky	5:1	5:1	6:1	10:1	12:1	14:1	15:1	15:1	20:1
	10	10	12	20	24	28	30	30	30
Louisiana	6:1	6:1	8:1	12:1	14:1	16:1	20:1	25:1	25:1
	NR	NR	NR	NR	NR	NR	NR	NR	NR
Maine	4:1	4:1	5:1	5:1	10:1	10:1	10:1	13:1	13:1
	12	12	15	15	30	30	30	NR	NR
*Maryland	3:1	3:1	3:1	6:1	10:1	10:1	15:1	15:1	15:1
	6	6	9	12	20	20	30	30	30
*Massachusetts	3:1/7:2	4:1/9:2	10:1	10:1	15:1	15:1	15:1		
	7	9	20	20	30	30	30		
Michigan	4:1	4:1	4:1	4:1	10:1	12:1	12:1	20:1	20:1
	NR	NR	NR	NR	NR	NR	NR	NR	NR
Minnesota	4:1	4:1	7:1	7:1	10:1	10:1	10:1	15:1	15:1
	8	8	14	14	20	20	20	30	30

Child to Staff Ratio and Group Size Requirements (by State)

State	Age of Children								
	6 wks.	9 mos.	18 mos.	27 mos.	3 yrs.	4 yrs.	5 yrs.	6 yrs.	7 yrs.
Mississippi	5:1	5:1	9:1	12:1	14:1	16:1	20:1	20:1	20:1
	10	10	10	14	14	16	20	20	20
Missouri	4:1	4:1	4:1	8:1	10:1	10:1	16:1	16:1	16:1
	8	8	8	16	NR	NR	NR	NR	NR
Montana	4:1	4:1	4:1	8:1	8:1	10:1	10:1	14:1	14:1
	NR	NR	NR	NR	NR	NR	NR	NR	NR
Nebraska	4:1	4:1	6:1	6:1	10:1	12:1	15:1	15:1	15:1
	NR	NR	NR	NR	NR	NR	NR	NR	NR
*Nevada	4:1	6:1	8:1	10:1	13:1	13:1	13:1	13:1	13:1
	NR	NR	NR	NR	NR	NR	NR	NR	NR
*New Hampshire	4:1	4:1	5:1	6:1	8:1	12:1	15:1	15:1	15:1
	12	12	15	18	24	24	30	30	30
New Jersey	4:1	4:1	7:1	7:1	10:1	12:1	15:1	18:1	18:1
	20	20	20	20	20	20	20	30	30
*New Mexico	6:1	6:1	6:1	10:1	12:1	12:1	15:1	15:1	15:1
	NR	NR	NR	NR	NR	NR	NR	NR	NR
New York	4:1	4:1	5:1	5:1	7:1	8:1	9:1	10:1	10:1
	8	8	10	10	14	16	18	20	20
NY City	4:1	4:1	5:1	5:1	7.5:1	12:1	15:1	15:1	N
	8	8	10	10	15	20	25	25	N
*North Carolina	5:1	5:1	6:1	10:1	15:1	20:1	25:1	25:1	25:1
	10	10	12	20	25	25	25	25	25
North Dakota	4:1	4:1	4:1	5:1	7:1	10:1	12:1	18:1	18:1
	NR	NR	NR	NR	NR	NR	NR	NR	NR
Ohio	5:1	5:1	7:1	7:1	12:1	12:1	18:1	18:1	18:1
	12	12	14	14	24	28	36	36	36
Oklahoma	4:1	4:1	6:1	8:1	12:1	15:1	15:1	20:1	20:1
	8	8	12	16	24	30	30	40	40
Oregon	4:1	4:1	4:1	4:1	10:1	10:1	15:1	15:1	15:1
	8	8	8	8	20	20	30	30	30
Pennsylvania	4:1	4:1	5:1	6:1	10:1	10:1	10:1	12:1	12:1
	8	8	10	12	20	20	20	24	24
Rhode Island	4:1	4:1	6:1	6:1	9:1	10:1	12:1	13:1	13:1
	8	8	12	12	18	20	24	NR	NR

Child to Staff Ratio and Group Size Requirements (by State)

State	Age of Children								
	6 wks.	9 mos.	18 mos.	27 mos.	3 yrs.	4 yrs.	5 yrs.	6 yrs.	7 yrs.
South Carolina	6:1 NR	6:1 NR	6:1 NR	10:1 NR	13:1 NR	18:1 NR	21:1 NR	23:1 NR	23:1 NR
South Dakota	5:1 20	5:1 20	5:1 20	5:1 20	10:1 20	10:1 20	10:1 20	15:1 20	15:1 20
Tennessee	5:1 10	5:1 10	7:1 14	8:1 16	10:1 20	15:1 20	20:1 20	25:1 25	25:1 25
Texas	4:1/ 10:2 10	9:1 18	13:1 26	17:1 34	20:1/ 35:2 35	24:1/ 35:2 35	26:1/ 35:2 35		
Utah	4:1 8	4:1 8	4:1 8	7:1 25	12:1 25	15:1 25	20:1 25	20:1 25	20:1 25
Vermont	4:1 8	4:1 8	4:1 8	5:1 10	10:1 20	10:1 20	10:1 20	13:1 NR	13:1 NR
Virginia	4:1 NR	4:1 NR	5:1 NR	10:1 NR	10:1 NR	12:1 NR	12:1 NR	20:1 NR	20:1 NR
Washington	4:1 8	4:1 8	7:1 14	7:1 14	10:1 20	10:1 20	10:1 20	15:1 30	15:1 30
West Virginia	NA to 12 wks.	4:1 NR	4:1 NR	8:1 NR	10:1 NR	12:1 NR	15:1 NR	16:1 NR	16:1 NR
Wisconsin	4:1 8	4:1 8	4:1 8	6:1 12	10:1 20	13:1 24	17:1 32	18:1 32	18:1 32
Wyoming	5:1 NR	5:1 NR	5:1 NR	8:1 NR	10:1 NR	15:1 NR	20:1 NR	25:1 NR	25:1 NR

KEY

NA = Not Allowed

NR = Not Regulated

N = Not Specified

* Additional details and specifications for these states are conditions to these requirements.

13

Parent's Notes

The Basics from the Director:

1. Hours of operation _____
2. Days closed _____
3. Full-time fees _____
4. Part-time fees _____
5. Deposit, registration, and other fees _____

6. Payment policy _____
7. Do you pay if out sick or on vacation? _____
8. Late fees and policy _____
9. Meals or snacks provided _____
10. Diapers and wipes provided _____
11. Can parents drop in at any time? _____
12. Sick policy _____

13. What do you do when children are ill,
    and you can't contact the parents? _____

14. What, if any, are parent requirements for participation? _____

15. What are your requirements for teachers? _____

16. What are your requirements for support staff, assistants, and caregivers? _____

17. Do you do criminal background checks? _____

18. What kind of background checks are done? _____

19. What is the retention rate for your staff? _____
20. How many teachers and caregivers are employed? _____
21. How long have most of them been here? _____
22. What is your background, and how long have you been at the center? _____

23. Is there ongoing staff training? _____
24. What topics are teachers trained in? _____

25. How many staff members have CPR and first-aid training? _____
26. How many children are in the center? _____
27. How many children are in my child's age group? _____
28. How are the children separated in the center (age groupings)? _____

29. What is the staff to child ratio for my child's age group? _____
29. What are the ratios for the rest of the center? _____
30. How does that compare to state qualifications? _____
31. How does that compare to NAEYC suggestions for ratios? _____
32. Are you NAEYC accredited or will you be pursuing NAEYC accreditation?
33. What is the educational philosophy of the center? _____

34. How are transitions handled? _____

35. What is your discipline philosophy? _____

36. How are sad children cared for? _____

37. What are the means for communicating with
    parents on a regular basis? _____

38. What is a typical day in my child's age group like? _____

39. What sets your center apart from others? _____

40. What emergency procedures are in place? _____

41. Could you give me the name and phone numbers
    of two or three parents in the center for reference? _____

Notes from Your Center Tour

Check off yes or no in each category.

Facility
Yes/No

Does the center appear clean? ☐ ☐
Does it smell clean? ☐ ☐
Are toys and materials in good condition? ☐ ☐
Are the furnishings in good condition? ☐ ☐
Are electrical outlets covered? ☐ ☐
Do you notice smoke alarms and fire extinguishers? ☐ ☐
Does the facility appear safe? ☐ ☐
Are the entrances to the center secure? ☐ ☐

Staff
Yes/No

Are teachers and caregivers providing individual
    attention to the children? ☐ ☐

Yes/No

Are they speaking kindly or firmly, rather than yelling
    at the children? ☐ ☐
Does the staff sit with the children in the different activities,
    instead of standing over them with arms crossed? ☐ ☐
Does staff appear affectionate and responsive toward
    the children? ☐ ☐
Do the children seem happy? ☐ ☐
Does the staff seem happy? ☐ ☐
Does the staff wash their hands before and after diapering
    and food preparation? ☐ ☐
Do the activities seem age appropriate? ☐ ☐
Would my child enjoy these activities? ☐ ☐

Playground

Yes/No

Does it appear safe? ☐ ☐
Is there enough room for all of the children? ☐ ☐

Gut instinct

Yes/No

Well? ☐ ☐

INDEX